LITERATURE AND SOCIAL CHANGE

LITERATURE AND SOCIAL CHANGE

Emerging Perspectives in Dalit Literature

Parmod Kumar Mehra

KALPAZ

ISBN: 978-93-5128-088-0

Price: ` 690

First Published, 2015

Published by

Kalpaz Publications
C-30, Satyawati Nagar,
Delhi - 110052
E-mail: kalpaz@hotmail.com
Ph.: 9212142040

Laser Typesetting: Rajender Vashist, Delhi
Printed at: Chawla Offset, Delhi

Cataloging in Publication Data—DK
Courtesy: D.K. Agencies (P) Ltd. <docinfo@dkagencies.com>

Literature and social change : emerging perspectives in dalit literature / Parmod Kumar Mehra.
pages cm
Contributed articles.
Includes bibliographical references and index.
ISBN 9789351280880

1. Indic literature—Dalit authors—History and criticism. 2. Social change in literature. 3. Marginality, Social, in literature. 4. Women in literature. I. Mehra, Parmod Kumar, editor.

DDC 891.4 23

This book is a tribute and dedicated to all Dalit literary figures and activists who have relentlessly supported and carried forward the cause of millions suffering in India in the name of caste and to Anu, Ryaan and Agatha whom I love and cherish with all my heart.

Contents

Preface

The church bell rang
Everyone entered in
The azaan heard from mosque
Everyone entered in
The bell of temple rang
Some entered in
And some stood out.

Dalit literature for a long time has largely been disregarded and not taken seriously in the literary circles. Now, it is increasingly being treated and used as a definite marker of Social Change or lack of it. Even after the publication of translations from modern Marathi literature entitled *Poisoned Bread* edited by Arjun Dangle with a prefatory note by Gail Omvedt had already sparked debates in the literary circles and Arun Prabha Mukherjee (York University, Toronto) who translated Omprakash Valmiki's *Joothan* (1997) into English in 2003 and wrote an introduction to it, the ideologically hardened attitudes are beginning to melt. The volume on Dalit writings from two south Indian states *No Alphabet in Sight* edited by Susie Tharu and K. Satyanarayana, opens up a new debate on the long history of Dalit literature and its current prominence in the contemporary scene of literature and politics. It also shows how Dalit literature moves beyond the usual discourses of literary modernity.

This collaborative effort based on Dalit Literary Studies is for anyone, in any context, who feels that there is a need to look at critical and alternative positions. Dalit is a word used for over four decades now and has gained great currency. The term 'Dalit' has emerged as a new theoretical and critical framework to check all kinds of discrimination. In the late twentieth century and early twenty first century, the world at large and literary scene in particular has witnessed an emerging pattern of expression and dissent, in an unprecedented manner and scale, from the People who were relatively subdued by now out against the discrimination and oppression of all kinds. These people constitute indigenous communities and women across the world. Dalits and Adivasis in India too figure prominently among those. This book is an academic platform to add to that process. As it is well known, Indigenous communities were not only at odds with political and economic colonialism right from the start, but also quarreled with hegemonic concepts of writing from the very moment the colonialists imported them into the country. As we already know that the Dalit discourse in India have occupied significant place in the discipline of literature as well as in the discourse of social sciences. Like any other socially active discourse, this is also dynamic and keeps engaging with newer ideas and themes. The literary expression of political consciousness and movements among or for the Dalits across India is the new emerging trend. This trend has served enormously to the cause and widened its constituency. The present book explores relationship between politics and literature with a critical analysis of texts from the Hindi literature both by Dalits and non-Dalits. It underlines not only the major issues and concerns of the literature but also to demonstrate that political consciousness is also expressed through many more innovative and creative methods like art and literature. This book also claims to be a provocative and thoughtful account of the debates among Dalit writers on how Dalit literature should be approached. These people have raised formidable voices calling for a substantial change that they, and their ancestors, have been subjected to, and demanding their right to play a central role in shaping communities, nations and the world at large. Their writings both in content and form defy the established and institutionalised order of literature. What is easily perceptible that there is a definite sense of celebration of their identities as well as an ethically driven theoretical framework to check the imbalances created over a period of time. This book is an anthology of critical research papers contributed by different scholars hailing from the different parts of India to take into account of trends and issues reflecting a perpetual dialogue coupled with a deep rooted sense of contestation. Heinz Werner Wessler from Sweden has also contributed significantly. Also, to take into account the strategies used by Dalit writers, and discuss the politics of reception and production. It contains number of scholarly papers dealing with the various aspects of Dalit Literature, *Chokamela* the pioneer of Untouchable Movement in Maharashtra, the growth and evaluation of Dalit literature, Dalit Literary theory, Dalit feminism, Dalit poetry, distincitve voices of distress, dalit historiography, the othered and unempowered by M.R. Anand, the Dalit sensibility in the writings of Jim Corbett, Gujarati Dalit poetry, reversing centrality and marginality. This book will be treasured not only by students but also by those who wish to study critically the dalit writings of the period. In addition, it will enrich readers' understanding of dalit and Indian literary history and culture.The present book successfully hints towards increasing realisation towards the importance of Dalit solidarity, a broader liberating alliance of the people subjected and exploited by Hindu colonisation for centuries. This is also acknowledged and emphasised that only such an emancipating alliance of the outcastes, women and non-elite minorities in India can effectively initiate social change, sustain democracy and resist cultural nationalism and fascism in Kerala and India in the 21st century. The challenges are complex and plural and so need to be the countering critical and democratic projects. This is the serious and strategic task ahead for the new Dalit critical writers. Each of these articles has been received with great applause during the three days International Conference which took place at Indira Gandhi National Open University from 20-22 February, 2013. All of these successfully trace the development of one or the other significant aspect of Dalit identity, both historically and in terms of literary contributions to its development. The chapter on Radical Feminism is mapped in the context of social, political and cultural development. In a nutshell, the book provides social, political, historical, literary contexts of the overall Dalit literature.

Parmod Kumar Mehra

Acknowledgements

I would like to express my gratitude to the many people who saw me through this *book*; to all those who provided support, talked things over, read, wrote, offered all support.

The real credit goes to all the contributors particularly Heinz Werner Wessler, Dr Putul Sathe, Mr Dinesh Misra, Dr Kanchan Verma, Dr M.B. Gaijan, Ms Runa Chakraborty, Shamali Gupta Bose, Siddaramu. B, Dr Saroj Mahananda, Dr Bolleddu Siva Nagaiah and, Mr Mridula Rashmi, Mr Bijender Singh and Ms Kalyanee Rajan. With their support, this book would prove to be a sustantial discourse on the subject and hopefully help in the process of finding tangible solutions to the long pending problem.

I sincerely acknowlegde these individuals for having taken time out to work for a enormously important theme. I would like to offer special thanks to the Prof Lynette Russel and Prof Sunaina Kumar as a whole for actively participating in the feedback and contributions for this book.

I would also like to extend my gratitude to Prof Rumina Sethi for her invaluable effort in guiding me through the whole process. I heartly appreciate all supports and acknowledge that the credit for the best outcome of the study goes to all supporters.

I would like to thank my family: my parents for nurturing me with true love and supporting me spiritually throughout my life and my wife Anu for standing beside me throughout my career. She has been my inspiration and motivation for continuing to improve my knowledge and move my career forward. She has offered true support and stood with me when it mattered most.

Kalpaz Publications also needs special mention for being a constant support. His interest for publishing socially significant titles brought us together.

Parmod Kumar Mehra

List of Contributors

Bolleddu Siva Nagaiah, Asst. Professor of English, Department of English Studies, Central University of Tamil Nadu, Thiruvarur, Tamil Nadu.

Dada. R. Dadas, Research Scholar School of Social Work, Tata Institute of Social Sciences, Deonar, Mumbai.

Dinesh Misra, President Emeritus, Indian Society of Authors.

Heinz Werner Wessler, University of Uppsala Sweden.

K. Anil Kumar, Asst. Professor, School of Social Sciences, Indira Gandhi National Open University, Maidan Garhi, New Delhi.

Kalyanee Rajan, Asst. Professor Department of English Daulat Ram College, University of Delhi.

Kanchan Verma, Lady Shri Ram College for Women, University of Delhi.

M.B. Gaijan, Department of English, Samaldas Arts College, Bhavnagar University Bhavnagar Mahasveta Devi, Torch-bearer of the Movement.

N.V. Sangvikar, Department of Communication and Journalism, University of Pune, Pune.

Parmod Kumar, Asst. Professor, Faculty of English, Indira Gandhi National Open University, New Delhi.

Putul Sathe, Department of English, SNDT College of Arts, SNDT Women's University, Mumbai.

Ranjith Thankappan, Assistant Professor, Department of Journalism and Mass Communication, School of Communication Studies, The English and Foreign Languages University, Hyderabad-500007.

Runa Chakraborty, Ph.D Scholar, University of Calcutta.

Saroj Mahananda, Jamia Millia Islamia University, North Delhi.

Shamali Gupta Bose, Head and Asst. Professor, Department of Mass Media, Ramnarain Ruia College, Matunga, Mumbai

Siddaramu, B., Research/Faculty Associate, Department of Social Work, School of Humanities and Social Sciences, Gautam Buddha University, Greater Noida, U.P.

1

Fictionalising Social Change: Violence and Non-violence in the Imaginary of Collective Transformation in Some Hindi Dalit Novels

Heinz Werner Wessler

"Writing a novel is not easy ..." writes Kapāṛiyā (1995) in the preface of his novel "The Oath on behalf of the earth".[1] More than a short story requires the novel requires a structured conception, a clear shape and an organised narrative. The primary and secondary characters have to be well designed, storylines developed, more or less complex narratives designed, dramatic and rhetorical devices applied. In other words, the production of a novel is bound to be an enduring process of conceptionalisation, writing, editing, and constant revision. While a short story or a poem can be written on the fly—regardless of its literary quality—a novel first requires long breath between the concept and the final draft. Spontaneity can be a feature in the writing of a short story and a poem, and it can be considered either as strength or weakness in the literary production or individual authors. The case of novels, however, is different. In novels, spontaneity comes at the expense of the unity of the characters and compelling conception of plots. In other words: The kind of narrativity of novels is necessarily very different from the reflexivity of shorter prose forms.

Often, moreover, the terminology is vague: Is the term "*Upanyās*"—a Sanskrit term adopted from Bengali in the 19th Century—appropriate for all kinds of fictional literature that exceeds a certain length? The literary histories of Hindi sometimes leave the reader with the impression that any fictional text from a certain number of pages onwards is categorised as a novel, irrespectively of any literary criteria. Sometimes the terms "*Lambī Kahānī*" ("long story") and "Upanyās" are treated almost as synonyms. Fictional prose texts once they have a certain length are mostly conveniently called Upanyās.[2]

It is however not my intention to go into the intricacies of the definition of literary genres in Hindi literature in this article. It can in general be said that while a large number of writers regularly produce short stories, short lyric forms and autobiographical texts, few dare to cross over to longer literary forms, especially the novel. The preference of the short form is at least partly related to prevailing reading behaviour on one side and the forms of publication on the other. Short forms of literature are easily consumable and they are easier to "accommodate" in magazines. Short stories are editorially easier to handle than long texts, which must be printed in several episodes. Journal editors can be reluctant to publish sequels. Besides, authors tend to believe that the novel is of less value since it is perceived that contemporary readership does not go for long texts. I personally have my doubts about this perception by the producers of literature, even though I came across this argument in discussions with a lot of authors. At least for the international market, this definitely is a false perception. On a worldwide scope the novel is the most successful genre of literature.

This may explain why the number of *Dalit* novels in Hindi is comparatively low, while the production of Hindi Dalit literature in general has seen twenty years extraordinary rich in output. In Jayprakāś Kardam's Dalit literature yearbooks, issued annually since 1999, only in the 2001 vintage, a single section of a novel (upanyāsaṃś) can be found. "*Apekṣā*", "*Yudhrat ām ādmī*" and other literary magazines with some focus on Dalit literature clearly have similar likings.

I don't want to go into the ever ongoing discussion on how to define Dalit literature from a perspective of contents analysis. However, there generally is a strong agreement that social transformation must be a central issue in any piece of Dalit literature. My focus in the following reading of Hindi Dalit novels is on how social transformation, which figures prominently in them, is fictionalised. I'll start with probably the earliest published Dalit novel in Hindi, "*Karuṇā*" of 1986

"Karuṇā" (Kardam 1986)

Rameś is happily married to Karuṇā. He has to stop his studies after the death of his father (pp. 7, 13) and provide a financial basis for the family. Shortly after, his mother dies and he himself is sterilised because he connects this decision with it in the hope for an employment offer as a teacher during the period of the emergency government (1975-1977; p. 14, see 67). Later, due to a traffic accident, he is even unable to consummate the marriage (p. 19). After a deeply moving encounter with a Buddhist nun who opens his eyes to the suffering nature of life in general, Karuṇā, after these blows of fate, and given the transience of the world secretly leaves her husband to herself to become a nun. When she departs, there is no despair on her face but only a "hope for peace" (p. 21).

Shortly after, Rameś has to face another blow. His sister Rita is rejected by her in-laws family over her continued barrenness after a few years of marriage. Rita sees no future for herself and creates additional grief by her suicide (p. 25).

In the following Chapter 4, Rameś is committed to achieve a judgement of the village council against Sūraj, son of the village mayor, who is accused of attempted rape of a Dalit girl and for his father, even the mild judgement to a two-year exile from the village for his no-good son lacks support. In the *Paṃcāyat* (village council) an opinion surfaces that the raping of a *Cḥamar* woman is not to be considered a particularly terrible offence.[3] Since Rameś has operated the indictment before the village council however, Sūraj is now full of hate (*kasak*) against him (p. 30).

In the city, Sūraj lives a life between booze and prostitutes that he can afford thanks to the stolen jewels of his dead mother (p. 52). As a revenge, he spreads out rumours that Rameś had poisoned his sister Rītā (p. 31). He bribes a police inspector who starts an investigation and arrests Rameś (p. 34). In the court, Rameś is promptly found guilty and sentenced to a long prison term (p. 40).

Without knowing anything about it, Karuṇā is a respected nun who is even elected to leadership positions in the religious hierarchy. She is active in fighting against negative developments of the order, like the exclusion of a lecherous monk, and especially the establishment of educational and health institutions (p. 37). Meanwhile Rameś thinks about his life in prison. Being completely disillusioned, he cannot follow the revolution fantasies of a fellow prisoner (S. 47). Society as a whole is completely corrupt for him and caught up in social traditionalism. Neither violence nor the silent endurance of exploitation and injustice can change society, as Rameś's prison perspective shows. He no longer shaves his face, his worldly appearance is no longer interesting for him (p. 42). He is completely disillusioned from his socially engaged activism, self-interest is prevailing everywhere (p. 45). Society does not leave traditional beliefs (p. 46), justice is only for the Mighty (p. 45), otherwise there is injustice prevailing (*anyāy*, p. 47). Even his belief in democracy (*loktaṃtr*) is shaken because his unjust conviction is possible (p. 66).

Sūraj also ends up in jail after he had been taken to task by his father because of his way of life out of fear for his political candidacy for state election, and killed him in drunken stupor (p. 53). "The most important thing is a loving heart!" (p. 54)—so is the deep knowledge of Buddhist Karuṇā, who remembers Rameś all of a sudden again, not knowing what has become of him (p. 56). Despite her ascent she wonders whether extraction (*palāyan*) from the world into monasticism is a form of cowardice (*kāyartā*, p. 57) or not. Karuṇā's parents have suffered from the time she disappeared, and even adopted a girl, who is to replace her, so to speak (p. 60). In his firm belief that Karuṇā has committed suicide, Rameś maintains his memories of his first wife in the prison of the district, including the more remote central prison in which he was transferred. He also mentions that it was Sūraj who then caused his arrest.

Meanwhile, the political state of emergency is terminated, the Congress Party under Indira Gandhi is deselected, but the new government after a short time proves to be disappointing as well (p. 68). Meanwhile Rameś is released from prison. Hardly in freedom, he reaches out the nearest Buddhist monastery where he fatefully meets his still beloved Karuṇā (p. 69), who convinces him to enter the monastic way of life. Both see their asceticism in the service of the "true religion" (*saddharm*), which is identical with ideal society (*ādarś samāj*, p. 71). At the end of the novel preaches Rameś—now the monk Ratnākar—on true happiness that is totally different from the promises of other religions.

Comment

According to my information from Jayprakāś Kardam, Karuṇā is the third novel written by him. The manuscripts of the first two novels, written in the 1970s, are -- according to the author -- lost with the publishers, who then delayed publication on purpose, or simply untraceable. Thus, the designation as a debut ("*prāraṃbhik udbhūti*") in the preface is only correct insofar as that this actually is the first published novel by Jayprakāś Kardam. Rām Anant notes in his preface, that "it is quite natural to discover aesthetic and artistic immaturity" in it (p. 2). He therefore refers the reader to a future work of the author, which will meet the needs of this more erudite reader (*rasagya pāṭhak*).

Kardam himself admits in his own preface frankly that this is the first attempt at writing a novel (*pratham prayās*, p. 4). Therefore, artistic maturity is not always guaranteed. Without the slightest hint of false vanity, he continues: "It is hoped that the learned reader's attention is not paid to the artistic shortcomings, but rather the basic course of the narrative. The suggestions of the readers will certainly be helpful to improve the level of future works." Even in person, Kardam has stressed again and again that he is willing to concede literary shortcomings not only in the early works, even in more recent publications. Of course it was necessary to develop literary quality, so Kardam, but the vanity of the individual author one should not give way to.

"Karuṇā" is created as a religious revival narration. In conversation expresses Kardam admits his deep involvement with Buddhism at the time of the writing - more than he could still be today. For Kardam Buddhism is a "way of life" (*jīvan ki paddhati*), "based on humanism" (*manuṣyatā par ādhārit*), Buddhism is a religion (dharm), which "is based on understanding and reason" (*buddhi aur vivek par ādhārit*), based on equality (*samāntā*, preface), but not on faith (*viśvās*). For Rameś, it seems there can be no better religion as "the religion of Buddhism and its theories" (*buddh kā dharm aur unke siddhāntoṃ se acchā*, p. 71).

In other words, Buddhism is a religion of enlightenment, of rationality, and dharm is contrary to *viśvās* – this statement is meant to be illustrated by the novel. Karuṇā's concern in the novel is therefore consistently: "The decline of men takes place exactly when he does not perceive reality." (p. 37). Through the "absence of science" (*vigyān ke abhav meṃhī*), he falls into the clutches of his (evil) desires (*vāsanā*, p. 37) – science and desires are oppositional. Therefore, the "true religion" (*saddharm*, pp. 37, 72) has to be spread out among common people, and this is what the monk Ratnākar fulfills in the end of the novel: His former desire for his beloved is transformed into asceticism and Buddhist preaching, which at the same time is to enlighten the common people. Karuṇā decides, therefore, to turn to missionary preaching. Rameś during his lonely prison days, explores the meaning of the Buddhist doctrine to the bottom; his prison cell is a kind of hermitage. In his reflections, vigyān leads to truth (p. 63). "Scientific spirit" (*vaigyāniktā*, p. 63) is the true ideal mindset.

Thus, modern education and the opening of health centers are two central goals of Buddhism, as represented by Karuṇā (pp. 39, 55). Rītā, however, indicates the failure of the individual facing the cruelty of society as such, and is made to leave the house of her in-laws.

On one hand, for Karuṇā and Rameś the world appears as vain and deceitful. On the other hand, however, this awareness is a kind of initiation into the transformation of personal desires in favour of higher social values and the idea of service for the spiritual, i.e., scientific upliftment of society. The dream of Rameś, after he turned away from the revolutionary ideas of his fellow prisoners is "a society based on the sense of justice (*nyāy*), equality (*samtā*) and fraternity (*bhrātṛtva*)" (p. 68). In place of the classical formula of democratic emancipation, freedom, equality and fraternity, the place of "freedom" is taken by "justice", which accommodates the Dalit cause better. In any case, Buddhism as presented in the novel is compatible to the ideals of the French revolution.

Similar to the narration in the novel "The Shack", Kardam follows two different types of actions in each chapter by chapter, as is very conventional in Hindi novels since Premchand: The biographies of Karuṇā and Rameś are followed up in consecutive chapters, and are joined together at the beginning and at the end. The novel begins with the married couple and ends up with both spouse become ascetics to spread the true religion.

In the novel, the "Buddhist community" on one hand is idealised: "There was nothing like dowry in the Buddhist community" (p. 23). The Buddhist community in general–and also in the contemporary India—that is quite different from the Hindu majority society with its ruinous dowry demands. On the other hand, the mother of the same Buddhist family that demands no dowry insults Rītā, when even after three years of marriage life, no sign of pregnancy appears, and thus forces her to return to their parents' home and ultimately drives her into suicide (p. 24). At the same time the non-Dalits are not only evil: Even for the bailiff, the buzz of his worthless son Sūraj goes too far, he's worried about his son (p. 29).

The archetype of the corrupt Brahmin occurs in the form of the police inspector Raghunāth Tivārī. Sūraj's bribing efforts which he refuses only initially under reference to dharm: "This is disregard of religious obligation (adharm) - I cannot participate in this" (p. 33). However, when given the money bundle that Suraj pulls out of his pocket, this initial refusal appears to turn out as a flirtatious attempt to drive up the price. "In front of the money, religious obligation (dharm) seemed pointless and lifeless" (p. 33)–a polemic statement on non-Buddhist dharm.

"The Shack" ("Chappar", Kardam 2003)

The novel narrates the story of a young and intellectually gifted Dalit man named Chandan. Chandan comes from the village of Mātāpur[4], where he grows up with his father Sukkhā and his mother Ramiyā under socially and economically miserable circumstances. Against the resistance of the village headman Ṭhakur Harnām Siṃh Sukkhā and the village priest Kāne Paṃḍit, Sukkhā takes care that his son goes to school and sends him, even though this proves to be economically difficult, to study in the nearby city for further studies, where Chandan is practically taken in like a son by an elderly Dalit man without family, who even supports him in financial distress. Chandan's dreams of city life are quickly disillusioned. Even in the city, he cannot escape poverty (p. 10). All kinds of new experiences permeate the young, inexperienced Chandan: The contrast between poor and better-off, the joy of folk music, the misery of drinking in cheap inns. His landlord and friend Hariyā—by profession a small toy sellers of commodities—turns out to be a good drinker.

One day, donations are collected in his living quarter to finance a public sacrifice. The collecting and donating activities initiate a critical reflection in Chandan: He starts to doubt the meaning of sacrifice, worship and religion altogether, and finally describes himself as an "atheist" (*nāstik*): "I do not believe in a self, a supreme self, not to power of a man or a God" (p. 18). Since he already has a certain impact on the people of his quarter, the people start to ponder: "Chandan says something right because, until now, we always come back here and worship God, but have we ever had some benefit of it?" (p. 19).

Chandan, looked after by Hariyā, continues to be devoted to his studies. Hariyā lends him even in a situation of financial crisis, audit fees that Chandan cannot afford (p. 56). In the rain and storm during the monsoon season, his attention suddenly turns to the torn and rotten clothes that Hariyā wears. All of a sudden the grinding poverty of his landlord becomes the focus of his attention. Hariyā, however, remembers his deceased young wife Rāmpyārī and sees in Chandan the son he would have liked to have from her (p. 23).

The narrative jumps back to the village in Chapter five and six, into the hovel of Chandan's parents and their concerns about the tax collection. The food is barely enough to survive - but the whole village is still affected by the scandal that Chandan as Dalit has migrated to the city to study (p. 30). The ruthless rule of castism (p. 31) has the village in its grip, that is why people turn against the idea of a Dalit boy going for higher studies. Sukkhā has to face the aversion of the village: "He has brought nothing but shame, this Sukkhā and his son!" (p. 33). Despite the constant hostility, Sukkhā's self-esteem has been awakened (*svābhimān jag gayā thā*, p. 35).

In Chapter seven, the narrative returns to the city. In college, he was initially the classic shy boy from the village, poor and even with a Dalit background - but over time he gets away with his feelings of inferiority (*hīntā kee bhāvnā*) and gains victory over his own shyness (*saṃkoc par vijay*, p. 36). In college Chandan makes his experiences an open discussion with members of the caste society. For example, Rāmhet argues that the "strength of will" (*icchāśakti*, p. 37) is the only way to success, but Chandan makes it clear that this position "is valid in reality for non-Dalits, not for Dalits" (p. 37). Important is "one's own progress" (*apnī unnati*, p. 38), especially in educational matters, because social emancipation is dependent on formation—a central message, which he tries to convey to people of his neighbourhood (p. 42). One's personal ethics are also important, including alcoholic abstinence (p. 41), so Chandan.

Chandan gets some extra income by opening a school for Dalit children. One day a very young mother named Kamlā wanted to enroll her son for lessons (p. 43). During registration, Chandan asks automatically for the father's name. It turns out that Kamlā had no husband, and the child has been conceived in a group raping (p. 47). Her secret hope is that her son, once grown up, should take revenge (p. 50).

In the village, Sukkhā's economic situation is on the decline. A mortgage on the house is a heavy burden, additional job opportunities as labourers with landowners no longer exist, because Sukkhā is literally excluded (p. 58). Rajnī, daughter of the mighty man in the village Ṭhākur Harnām Siṃh, develops unexpected sympathies for Chandan and his father, and tries to convince her own father to create opportunities for Sukkhā without much avail (p. 66ff). Rajnī and Chandan have once been classmates, she knows under what hardships and discrimination by classmates and teachers Chandan has managed to finish school, and she highly appreciates his perseverance and his sincerity (p. 67).

Chandan learns about Hariyā's tragic biography (Chapter 12, p. 71ff), which includes the early death of his wife and the rape and disappearance of his daughter. As Hariyā seeks police persecution of the instigator of the rape, he ends up in jail himself. After being set free he takes the law into his own hands and murders the main culprits with a chopping knife-but manages to cover up his complicity (p. 73). The daughter, pregnant by rape, flees home and never returns, much to Hariyā's disappointment. Chandan realises that Kamlā is Hariyā's daughter. Father and daughter are reunited in an dramatic scene through Chandan's mediation. Kamlā moves back to her father. Chandan wants to clear the space for her and move out himself, but on Hariyā's urging appeal, he decides to stay. Chandan is becoming more integrated into the urban Dalit society and is committed to increasing the educational training of Dalits.

Meanwhile Mātāpur is witnessing profound changes (Chapter 13, p. 81ff). Rajnī turns to be an advocate of Dalit interests in the village assembly (p. 82). She took charge of the correspondence between Chandan and his parents (who cannot write), which leads to a certain confidentiality and finally signals of love for Chandan, at the same time she becomes more and more critical of the power relations in the village. She eventually openly takes party for the untouchables, when the caste Hindu party discusses what to do against the progress in education of the Dalits in the village. Soon she also denies the marriage proposal according to her father (p. 91), while her relationship with Sukkhā and Ramiyā develops. With Rajnī's help, Sukkhā gets his farmland back, which had been retracted because of tax liabilities (p. 100).

During a visit in Mātāpur, delicate bonds of love between Rajni and Chandan become manifest. In Chapter 16, the transformation of Mātāpur towards an egalitarian society and the social emancipation of Dalits become reality. Inspired by Hariyā, Chandan visits his parents in the village once again (p. 101). It turns out to his surprise that not only education has progressed well in the village, but also the soil was now divided among the landless and untouchability is no longer practiced.

Kāne Paṃḍit, the village priest, left the village, Harnām Si ṃh waives his privileges and even starts tilling his soil himself after Sukkhā restrains him from a suicide attempt (Chapter 17). This goes so far that he doesn't like to be addressed by his caste indicating family name "Siṃh". Chandan insists on a non-violent attitude in the struggle for justice and equality (p. 107). The basis of social harmony should be "humanism" (manuṣyatā) and not the Hindu caste system. "Only humanism is our clan relationship, only humanism should make up our mutual relationship, and only religious humanism is our right!" (p. 112). The Ṭhākur has distributed his land to the poor (p. 112).

Comment

Jay Prakas Kardam's "Chappar", his second published novel, first appeared in 1994, the changes in the "enhanced edition" (*saṃśodhit saṃskaraṇ*) of 2003 concern improvements of the numerous misprints of the first edition. "The Shack" is considered his major work and has been variously and erroneously referred to as the first Dalit novel in Hindi. The title refers to the dwelling of Sukkhā that is returned to him after its retraction and after the inner transformation of Harnām Siṃh, the departure of the village priest and the deep transformation of social conditions in the village (p. 99).

The first great spiritual advancement of Chandan is his upcoming doubt in the traditional religion in Chapter 3 (pp. 16-20). He expresses his doubts openly and soon turns into an atheist, which has its immediate effect on the people in his neighborhood, i.e., the Dalit community. The public expression of his doubt, the implementation of collective experience in personal knowledge is part of the breakthrough itself.

All change starts with the education efforts of Chandan. This makes him into a kind of cultural hero, with a deep impact on the village as a whole. At first he develops self-esteem, the inborn feelings of inferiority and shyness pass away. The defender of the established order and the most powerful man in the village, Ṭhākur Harnām Siṃh, already questioning his own social identity, asks himself what to do with his power, when all village inhabitants begin "a life of self-sufficiency and self-respect" (p. 66) in the village. His daughter Rajnī is for him the embodiment of reason and enlightened conscience, responds to his doubt: "But Father, these are human beings! Is that about right if someone exploits the others?" (p. 66). Rajnī knows that it is not easy to explain to her own father to let go his privileges as feudal lord, even though they don't really make him happy. Rather, he emphasises initially that power (*varcasva*) and identity (*asmitā*, p. 66) are closely linked to his stand.

However, the most astonishing part of the plot is that the improbable becomes possible—a process of internal transformation of evil into good. This fits the Buddhism-shaped declaration of Chandan that the answer to violence (*hiṃsā*) should not be counter-violence but nonviolence (*ahiṃsā*, p.107). "We are against the social conditions, not against individual persons" (p.109) is the message of the cultural hero, which even brings the Ṭhākur to repentance. The transformation is first and foremost mental, and secondarily social: After the despair and the attempted suicide follows in an inner clarification process of repentance and inner cleansing—with support Sukkhās as agents of human kindness, of forgiveness granted to the Ṭhākur, which thus helps him to overcome the pangs of conscience: "The traditional religion (dharm) of the people is an error!" (p. 111). The bad character achieves the true "turn of heart", changes his complete life disregarding his personal interests (or, in the terminology of the first novel Karuṇā, "desire") and turns into a messenger of truth and social harmony.

The social optimism in the novel is probably one of the most memorable examples of utopian thinking in modern Hindi literature altogether. In Chapter 17 of the novel, the conflict between the bailiff and the discriminatory system for which he stands, and the world of simple farmers and the Dalits in particular takes a dramatic turn. The author describes here his vision of transforming the traditional village social structure in an egalitarian, non-discriminatory society—a utopian design far away from both the politics of the day as well as the continuing discriminatory structures in society. Hiṃsā and ahiṃsā are structural terms, they mark the discourse on two different ways of dealing with society and conflict. The focus is not so much on justice, human rights or social uplift, but on a kind of profound change starting on the level of beliefs and consciousness deep inside the human being.

Education is the silver bullet for social emancipation in

society as a whole and at the same time catalyst of solidarity within the Dalit community. In the urban school that Chandan starts, those who have learned to read and write immediately start to spread their knowledge to others who have not yet learned the alphabet. As a result of this educational offensive, Dalits come slowly out of the shadows of lack of education (*aśikṣā*) and ignorance (*agyān*, p. 76). The movement for social change (*sāmājik badlāv*) begins with this momentum – education is not a result of the social change, but its cause. The decisiveness (*saṃkalp*) and asceticism (*tyāg*) of Chandan as a promoter of the emancipation plays a central role in the motivation of Hariyā's (p. 78), as well as his strength (*dṛṛhtā*) and his inner fire (*andar ki āg*, p. 80). Chandan is the Dalit cultural hero per se.

The aim is to replace castism by "humanism" (*mānavvād*, p. 95, manuṣyatā, p. 112), justice and equality (nyāy aur samtā) - the conditions (*vyavasthā*) that produce injustice and inequality (avyāy aur asmāntā p. 109) must be changed. This "humanism" triggers from Hinduism as a living value system. Because of "humanism" (*manuṣyatā*) and because of sociability (*sāmājiktā*) man cannot ignore the pain and suffering of others (p. 46). Towards the end of the novel features some kind of metaphysical Buddhism in Kamlā's death, when Hariyā the non-educated Dalit hero—comforts Chandan about the death of his own daughter (with whom Chandan had developed some kind of platonic love relationship): "Whoever is born, certainly has to die" (p. 118). In the face of death, Buddhism has a comforting function that "humanism" on its own cannot have.

"The Oath in the Name of the Earth" (*Miṭṭī kī saugaṃdh*, Kapāṛiyā 1995):

This novel features a "justice force" (nyāy *senā*, p. 49ff) for the revenge of the Dalits against oppression, murder and rape. The village headman Mohan Siṃh is a rapist and brutal oppressor, declared to be a descendent of Rāvaṇ (p. 9) by the Dalits, but his younger son Vijendra Siṃh is "honest" (*Śarīf*, p. 9). He takes care of Śīlā, who has been raped by his own father, and initiates a police inquiry into the case. This and his plan to marry her lead to severe quarrels within the family, while the Dalit policeman Jagjīvan starts recruiting a "justice force" to defend the Dalits and to take the law in their own hands, for example by castrating rapists. Vijendra Siṃh becomes the head of the "justice force", while his father hires his own men to ignite the Dalit quarter (p. 55). A police inquire has to face all kinds of obstructions, and finally the superintendent has no chance against a corrupt magistrate, who has been bribed by the village headman. When Vijendra finally manages to convince his father of the marriage with Śīlā, his grandmother gradually poisons his bride in order to prevent a pregnancy (p. 87). Vijendra and Śīlā have to fled away to the town to avoid the violent interventions of the family (p. 91), and within short her pregnancy is revealed (p. 97). In a final showdown, the "justice forcc" together with police forces prevent Vijendra's father and his men to kill Śīlā, which leads to Mohan Siṃh arrest and the courts decision on a punishment of ten years in prison. In the end, Vijendra returns to the farm together with his wife—and forgives the head of his father's men, Kaluā, who would like to marry Vijendra's sister Kamlā—which Vijendra gladly supports in an act of reconciliation.

Comment

Rape, an unscrupulous landowner and village headman, and a mixed marriage between a Dalit and the off spring of the leading person in the village strongly remind Jayprakāś Kardam's second novel. Mohan Siṃh, the local feudal lord, is completely unscrupulous, the villain *per se*. He is ill-tempered, has constant guards around him who are ready to carry out any kind of action on order (with unclear social background), he consumes alcohol (p. 7), is constantly on search for sex, but not particularly intelligent. The ingenious plan to allow Vijendra and Śīlā to marry, but to get Śīlā poisoned in order to keep her barren, comes from the equally ruthless grandmother, but he instantly goes for it. Śamendra is also completely unscrupulous, sleeps with prostitutes and drinks alcohol (p. 13)–again the full profile of a wicked personality. "Between the great lord and small lord [i.e., between the two brothers] is a difference like between heaven and earth" (p. 17). The younger son of the landowner however has compassion (*dayā*, p. 17), unlike the elder, and displays only but the features of a moral character. It is interesting how alcohol consumption is invariably attributed to the bad. There is no attempt to explain how this uneven balance of good and bad qualities within one family could have developed.

The good and the bad guys are distributed among many levels within the hierarchy. Thinking in caste categories is alien to the younger—in complete contrast to his older brother. The Ṭhākur insults Dalits according to his likings—in view of the allegations of the police inspector Jagjīvan it becomes clear, that the police uniform does not prevent him from discrimination: "How can there be an insult to somebody who has no honorable status at all?" (p. 36). For Vijendra, however, such references to caste status are an "insult to humanity" (*mānavtā kā apmān*, p. 44)–he even maintains his argument against the unscrupulous grandmother.

The wicked guys address the Camārs constantly as "*Harijan*"—in the sense of Mahatma Gandhi attribution, "children of God", occasionally they switch over to the not much more charming "scheduled caste" (*anusūcit jāti*, p. 14). The Ṭhākur instructs a farmer who asks him for a loan and says that he lives in the Dalit quarter that he should say "Harijan-quarter" (p. 56). Only in the closing speech of the Ṭhākur, he first speaks of the "Harijan woman", then the "Dalit woman" - Śīlā is meant—whom he is not ready to accept as daughter-in-law (p. 108ff). The drunken Kaluā says: "The damned Chamār ... has become an inspector ..." (p. 67). Vijendra, the ideal landlord, announces, however, that nobody can touch Gaṃgā—who had prostituted herself for Śamendra before (*chū bhī nahīṃ saktā*, p. 30), she is above her humiliation.

The fight is not only against discrimination, but also against hierarchic structures and their rhetoric. As the wife of Vijendra, the poor Dalit girl changed into a mistress—Śīlā asks the servant not to call her "mistress" (mālik, p. 98). As in the case of Gaṃgā, Vijendra is the ideal gallant cavalier and puts the highest moral motivation on display: the protection of his wife is his first duty (*pahlā dāyitva*, p. 99), he proudly proclaims.

It is striking that religion appears only indirectly if at all in the novel. While Kardam makes clear statements on the moral superiority of Buddhism, Kapāṛiyā avoids any remark that could be taken as an offence against Hindu beliefs or practices. Given the threat of arrest for raping Śīlā, the Ṭhākur uses an image from the Krishna mythology to make it clear how he will destroy the police inspector Jagjīvanrām: "Before the snake can raise her bonnet over me, I crush it" (p. 35)—an allusion to the popular Kāliyādaman episode in the biography of Krishna: The Divine Child Krishna dancing on the snake demon deemed invincible. The Ṭhākur sees himself in the role of the Almighty. However, this is only a rhetorical reference without any structural meaning. The younger son is in a conflict between his family loyalty, which he perceives in terms of "kartavya" (duty) and an "*adhikār*" (right based on values, p. 43). He even apologised to the grandmother that he cannot follow her orders (p. 45). He wants to bring Śīlā into the house in full honour, and somehow the agreement of his father is very important for his luck. Even though he argues and acts against his father and his interests, he does not question the social value system as such. He is a moralist in the strongest sense.

The most striking ideological difference to "Chappar" is the belief in violence. The objective of the "justice army" (nyāy senā, pp. 52, 60) is "war for justice" (nyāy *yuddh*, p. 60). As Śīlā proposes escaping, Vijendra emphasised that this fight (*saṃghars̩*) has to be fought out for the benefit of the poor (p. 61). His deeper motive is the totally unselfish love, which comes to the surface when he talks to the inspector: "Inspector ... isn't it possible that a person ... simply loves another person?" (p. 61), which means universal love to all human beings. But this love includes forming a militia, and to enforce justice with the means of robbery and violence. No trace of doubt on choosing the right means for the right course becomes visible, no inner conflicts, no remorse—as long as the purpose of action is the liberation of Dalits. The justice army wants rather simply responds to attacks, "smashing faces" (*mumh-tod* p. 72). The level of aggression is high, and justification is taken for granted. The militia as such, its acts and its motifs of action, are idealised—and it has all rights to take over the law in its own hands, since the police is incapable.

Beyond that there is no explanation why the younger son of the landlord turns away completely from his wicked family and even turns into the head of the justice army—and he turns even into the head of the justice army. It is no problem that the agency moves away from the Dalits to one of the Ṭhākurs.

Similarly to "Chappar", the good Ṭhākur figures prominently in the novel: While in "Chappar" the bad guy is transformed from evil to good after a crisis which brings him to the brink of suicide, there is no development of the characters in Prem Kapāṛiyā's novel. Violence plays an important role in all parts of living in the village—and the ideal is to rule out discriminative violence through the violence of the justice army. Unjustice (anyāy) is more a metaphor than a terminus technicus: A term that collects everything in the village that is discriminating for Dalits, including direct violence, the exploitation of the tillers, sexual violence from rhetorical intimidation to rape, and the prevention of Dalits from education. The central message of hope however is that violence is eliminated by organised counter-violence. The state power and its organ, the police, is deeply rooted in the social structure and its inherent discrimination in the village. The courts are irrelevant, politics are irrelevant—direct action alone is the clue to a solution of the problems of Dalits.

"When it becomes Morning" (*Jas tas bhāī saver, Satyaprakāś,* 1998).

In the center of the novel is the prototypical North Indian village, and in particular the psychological and economic dependence of a Dalit extended family to the completely unscrupulous village mighty Chaudharī Devīpāl and the temple priest Bhagat Harsannā, the growing Dalit solidarity and awareness of Dalit identity and the following just punishment of landowners and priests.

The action begins in the monsoon season 1990. At the beginning of the novel, the Dalit brothers Saravan and Haṃsā are introduced. While Haṃsā and his wife are deeply religious (p. 19 etc.), Saravan is enlightened and a rationalist to the core. He sees no point in religious ceremonies and vows. His brother Haṃsā refuses his attitude, throws his brother out of the house and after a fight completely withdraws himself away from him (pp. 11, 19). While this happens, a certain Chaudharī, full of "bestial instinct" (*paśu pravṛtti*, p. 11) harasses, rapes, and murders one of three grass cutting ladies, while the other two have to witness this passively out of fear. Under force, they even lend helping hands to throw Dhusiyā's body into a well.

Meanwhile, the young bank employee Śivdās lives in Delhi, where protests against the implementation of the Mandal Commission to provide quotes from government jobs for OBCs (Other Backward Classes) are being held (p. 22). His friends are urban intellectuals, including university lecturers, in which, in all modesty, he represents the Dalit position as such and is at the same time an advocate of the "secular", and patriotism in particular. Śivdās defends the advanced reservation policy among his acquaintances and friends (see pp. 52, 66). The intellectuals pretend to understand and support the Dalit position, they understand themselves as progressivists and praise mixed caste marriages (p. 70), etc.,—but at the end of the discussion, the discriminatory resentment comes to the surface: "You are an enemy of our society—and Sumedhā is still a child!" (p. 71). Śivdās' high caste girl friend Sumedhā who is willing to marry him (which Śivdās first postpones, p. 44), is summoned from her parents to Kānpur. Both have no idea that Prof Datt has informed her parents about her love relationship with a Dalit and has pushed them to quickly marriage off her daughter. Prof Datt later tried to dissuade Śivdās of his connection with Sumedhā. In the beginning, he appears to be sympathising with Śivdās as Dalit, and he also marks support for the marriage between different castes, but he finally accuses him of destroying Sumedhās luck because he was finally from low caste origin (p. 69).

In between the story of the village deity Jāharvīr and the Queen Bāchal (p. 30ff) forms part of the ongoing narration. Haṃsā's wife Sunahrī is in trance possessed by the goddess (p. 34), while the Chaudharī compels the grass cutter Rāmratī sexually and removes her seven year old son Munnā, as he becomes the witness of his sexual harassment (p. 47). The corrupt police uncovers Chaudharīs crimes (p. 50). Śivdās in the meantime applies for a position in the newly opened bank branch in the village. Hamsā and Saravans father Maṃgal Pahalvān recommend him paternally, but with a threatening undertone in his direction, warning him not to transfer urban perspectives to the village (p. 52). When his son falls ill, Haṃsā makes a spirit responsible for the disease. Saravan cannot convince him by rational arguments (p. 60ff). Haṃsā hates his brother more and more (p. 71), and driven by his money problems agrees on a suggestion of the Chaudharī, to pretend having been victim of a theft performed by his brother Saravan (p. 73). Saravan is then beaten up by the community and arrested by the police (pp. 76-77).

As Sumedhā doesn't return, Śivdās decides to look for her on his own in Kanpur, where he can make her actually out and meet her secretly (p. 78ff). It turns out that Sumedhā is to be married to a particularly unpleasant nephew of Prof Datt. Sumedhā is looking forward to the tragic fate of a forced marriage to a young man with bad character—he eats both meat and fish, and he is committed to the drinking of alcohol. Accepting her fate, she has already accepted, but is grateful to meet Śivdās one last time for a farewell and to have at least one time in life sexual intercourse with him (p. 84ff). When the family of Sumedhā learns on Śivdās' presence, it provides thugs to get him out of the way—Śivdās has to flee away from Kanpur to save his life (p. 86).

Back in the village, Śivdās has to suffer from discrimination, is highly engaged to bring the Chaudharī to court, but the witnesses are intimidated. In the celebration of Independence Day (August 15) Caudharī makes Maṃgal Pahalvān to an honorary chairman of the event in the village. Numerous guest speakers, predominantly Brahmins (p. 96), the basic tenor is the polemics against the caste based quota system. Reservation due to the economic situation—not the caste status—is being touted as an alternative. Finally, one of the speakers praises the caste as an organising order for a just society, and finally a resolution against the reservation policy is formulated and accepted (p. 99). Śivdās surprisingly gets permission to speak and is the only speaker who dares to defend the caste-wise reservation for Dalits and for low cast members in a way that everyone can understand, for which he is pelted with sandals and eggs (p. 101ff). Even with his "secular" nationalism, he fails to get the village community behind him (p. 104). As a result of this event, he is identified as an instigator by Chaudharī and is put in prison under false allegations (p. 109).

Chaudharī has long been keeping an eye on the 30-year-old wife of his devoted Haṃsā, Sunahrī. He impels Bhagat Harsannā, to let the pious Sunahrī one evening come to the temple for an exorcism in favour of her son, where a specially prepared ritual gift (Prasād, p. 111) mixed with a drug is given to her, which makes her subservient to desires (p. 109). After the rape, her husband Haṃsā rushes to the temple, where he silently listens to a conversation of Harsannā and Chaudharī, in which he mercilessly reveales that for him, religion is only but an instrument of power (p. 114). He immediately recognises that his brother Saravan is right. He then rushes to the home of Chaudharī, but is already expected of his followers and terribly beaten up (p. 116).

Maṃgal Pahalvān is meanwhile together with Rūplāl (father of Pahalvāns daughter) on a tour that brings him to "*dīkṣā bhūmi*" in Nagpur (Maharashtra), where Dr Ambedkar converted to Buddhism in 1956 (p. 117). When he returns, he gets angry and calls the followers of his wrestlers' club together. Jointly, they overcome the Chaudharī as well as Bhagat Harsannā, has them beaten up and the temple demolished (p. 120ff). The group returns to criminal action and reflects their situation. Haṃsā and Saravan are reconciled. Maṃgal Pahalvān summarises the event, saying that the banyan tree has to be felled so that another plant that will grow from under it, which should not get stunted in his shadow (p. 123).

In the middle of this, Chaudharī, Harsannā and their followers penetrate with truncheons against Dalits before and want to take revenge, but are repulsed. When the police arrives, which all of a sudden is now taking care of Law and Order (p. 126), Harsannā Chaudharī is arrested. The inspector has understood that "the measure of sin is full"—"the right will work out on itself" (p. 126). After a long night comes the day with its light—Maṃgal Pahalvān is now convinced by Rūplāl to flee away from the darkness—and to worship the shining light—a state like with the banyan tree, which has to fall. "When the eyes rise, the morning has come," remarks Rūplāl (p. 128).

Comment

The language of the author is much more sanskritised than the language of many other Dalit authors. At one point in the book enters the omniscient author with a direct address to the reader: "And, yes, there is one thing I forgot to tell the readers" (p. 58). The author addresses the reader that Sumedhā is a caste Hindu, while Śivdās is a Dalit. This connection kind of inter-caste marriage, says the author, happens only once or twice per century (p. 59)—which is probably exaggerating, even though it is true that this kind of marriages are indeed rare. The identification of author and Śivdās is obvious—at one point (p. 69), the author jumps from the third to the first person: "I said . . ." (instead Śivdās said).

Caste Hindus with the exception of Sumedhā—are characterised by more or less brute force and absolute ruthlessness. But even within the Dalits, armed violence erupts quickly. Besides, the police beats, tortures, blackmails. However, dispute within the Dalit society is instigated from the outside: Individual members of the community are deceived. Śivdās and Saravan are the only ones that cannot be seduced, because they are autonomous in judging and action. They embody idealistic humanism enlightenment, critique of religion and genuine love and readiness for personal martyrdom—and they are ready to forgive. In other words, they are perfect moral heroes.

At the same time, the description of evil groom Sumedhās in Kānpur, the nephew of Prof Datt, reveals Hindu middle class values and the full scale of their class judgments: He is a young man of bad character, drinks alcohol, eats meat and fish, raises covetous glances to his bride (p. 82).

The contrast between the hardly covered sexual greed of unscrupulous Chaudharī extremely delicate and erotic tension between Śivdās and Sumedhā mark the contrast between "animal instinct" and the ability to contain each other, "observed limits". In a particular moment of growing intimacy, Sumedhā's friends Sīmā ("limit") and Rekhā (line, p. 47) appear and mark the control of desires among Dalits. Only in the immediate image of her forced marriage, Sumedhā decides to cross that line and to sleep with Śivdās, which is described in a subtle way (p. 85)—the content of this social taboo breaking correlates with the severity of the emotional resignation of Sumedhā in a very traditional form of female passivity. The loyalty to the family is a similar ordeal as the martyr of Saravan and her friend Śivdās. Sumedhā's highly idealised love summons herself "martyr and holy" (*mere satitva va pavitra prem*, p. 86). The idealisation of feminine feelings is also noticeable in Sunahrī, who even after the insidious sexual abuse has pity with the women in the household of Chaudharī. She tries to call the abusive men to reason (p. 121).

Hindu beliefs and practices are an expression of consciously used hypocrisy in the novel—a religion the author portrays with bitter cynicism. Chaudharī Devīpāl and Harsannā Bhagat act only with the "fruit of action" in view: "The two men thought it was pointless to perform any action without the desire for a result. Bhagatjī spreads out the teaching of the Bhagavadgītā regarding the action without desire for results (p. 109)—hollow words, which have no meaning for his personal ethics. This remark is the introduction of the chapter of the ruthless seduction of religious Sunahrī. Harsannā whispers the "guru mantra" into Chaudharī's ear (p. 111), the secret initiatory verse—namely that Sunahrī is under drugs and he can misuse her now. Harsannā clarifies: "The fear of satanic powers is only but our net (with which we capture the pious), my friend!" (p. 114).

The vengeance however is cruel as well, as namely, Maṃgal Pahalvān demolished the temple with his followers: "Should the asshole but call a deity or something to help" (p. 155). The author lets his anger at this demolition as a writer dreamed of—a counter-violence fantasy that probably would instantly cause a national outcry if real. The banyan tree as a symbol of Hinduism, which must be taken so that other plants can grow in its shadow (p. 123) is in this understanding a rather radical fantasy, featuring nothing less than violence and revolution. In all mixes radical Enlightenment critique of religion. "If the son is not doing well or because of economic hardships it seems as if the wrath of God was to blame" (p. 123).

In contrast to the "state under the banyan tree, which is equal to the black night" (p. 128) the light (*prakāś*) appears—it is rationalism (*buddhivād*) to spread and leave darkness behind. "Therefore, we must destroy the myths that are prevalent in the society" (p. 128) emphasises Rūplāl in a programmatic statement at the end of the novel–which seems to be the *summa* of the novel. When all of a sudden, the truth turns into a powerful movement, the previously corrupt and brutal police village is suddenly reversed. As Śivdās is released from prison, the guard officer sees everything from a new perspective. "On the part of the police you will get support in order to achieve justice" (p. 127). At once the conditions are changed. The novel thus opens up a highly enlightened and idealistic light symbolism that recurs in the title that proclaims in Braj dialect: "When it becomes morning." At the end of the novel, the morning sun breaks through the long history of suffering with its splendor.

In Satyaprakāś (1998), the classical combination of classic storylines in town and country, as in some of Premchands novels and Godān in particular, clearly structures the ongoing plot. Similarly to Chandan in Jay Prakas Kardams novel "Chappar", Śivdās embodies the traveler between worlds, coming from the city to the village and has to accept Maṃgal Pahalvān's council or perhaps more precise—threat: "Now do not do so as you were here like in the city, my son," (p. 52). Not only for the city but for Dalits in general, different standards are established—when an official from the "experienced, qualified company" (p. 105) makes a mistake, it doesn't matter so much—but in case of the Dalit official, an error is unforgivable. Discrimination is and remains a universal reality—especially among the intellectual caste Hindus, who go for modern discourses, but basically operate an agenda in support of the caste society—as with Prof Datt or the many speakers with clearly identifiable Brahmin names during the independence day celebration.

The perhaps most interesting narratives of the novel are woven into the plot discussions about the reservation policy at the University of Kanpur (pp. 66-71), the speeches at the village celebration of Independence (pp. 96-101) and the following long rebuttal of Śivdās on egalitarianism and (secular) national pride cites (p. 104). In the first debate at the University of Kanpur, initially an understanding of the emancipation concerns of the Dalits appears to prevails, but the whole discussion boils down to that Prof Datt wants to convince Śivdās to abandon Sumedhā, where he openly puts forward the caste origin as the final argument—while at the same time, he follows a hidden agenda, since he wants to marry off Sumedhā to his own nephew.

Chairman of the Independence celebration—appointed by Chaudharī—is astonishingly Maṃgal Pahalvān, father of Saravan and Haṃsā - a Dalit who accepts this honor thankfully and proud, the prototypical Dalit coopted by Brahman society. Beyond that, abuses of "Harijan Act" are to be avoided (pp. 96-97). Dr Śivprasād declares to fight against "injustice" (anyāy) to the last breath (p. 98). "Anyāy" but is a central concept in the criticism of the caste by Dalits: The objective is the fight against social injustice. The same speaker goes so far as to claim that the idea of caste thinking has ceased to exist (p. 98). He then sets out to call for a joint resolution, whereupon Śivdās insists on his right to speak and politely contradicts. Finally he even quotes the doctrine of reincarnation as such, what his counterpart picks up in the style of a pupil's question to be explained, like a good student questionnaire and ends up with a sermon in favour of a society of the four Varṇas (castes).

Some General Comments on Novels in Hindi Dalit Literature

The narrative structure of the framework actions in the novels presented here is similar in each case: There is a clear cut linear time, parallel narrations follow up each other, and the perspective is that of a all-knowing author. There is not much suspension, hardly any subject change, and a kind of black-and-white setup of characters. Different parallel narratives are bundled together, like in "Chappar" different storylines parallel in town and countryside—penetrated by a clearly recognisable, linear arrow of time. The authorial narrative situation is always clear: The outsiders, omniscient narrator tells continuously from the overview perspective of the people involved in the third person.

The inner side of the central characters remains pale, a self-discovery of the narrative "I" hardly features prominently.

Love, hate and other emotions are serious, but a crisis of conscience does not happen. Interior monologues or narratives that form indirect discourses are almost entirely missing. Where they occur, they have a didactic-pedagogical connotation. Even in love affairs, which play a central role in all the novels, the external aspects of the events dominate. In the ascetic renunciation of the raped woman and single mother Kamlā, Chandan finds a basis to favour Rajnī in "Chappar". She is more of a passive sufferer and fits very much in the traditional role of the passive female, who does hardly claim agency.

History of the Dalits is martyrdom, they are predestined to fatalistic martyrdom, while Chandan is the hero of Dalit solidarity and liberation. Erotic feelings play an important role, but are just extremely cautious indicated, the irresistible, pressing for marriage and fulfilled in marriage and offspring love the caste boundaries the actual image and the epitome of "humanism", the breaking the caste barriers and they direct their hopes.

Central to this is the concept of dignity (*svābhimān*), how to regain and protect it. In Satyaprakāś (2000), the identification of the author is split with (male) characters on two main characters: Śivdās, the urban Dalit who decides for life in the village and in which the meet him beating suspicion given its bold anti speech at the independence ceremony turns into open hatred and physical aggression—the other Saravan, who has freed himself within the village of every faith and superstition, and with its commitment to rationalise worldviews his pious brother, his wife and even his father is deadly enemies to end up right to keep.

Kapāṛiyā 1995 falls here a little out of line, because the hero is not a Dalit: Ironically, the son of the extremely wicked Ṭhākur is the male role model, which is a member of the warrior caste from a land-owning family, who is raped to the father of his own. The Chāmar girl Śīlā let her love develop against all social convention, the intrigues and aggressive appetites murder of his father, marriage and marriage. And this is because his son Vijendra has turned into the leader of the "Justice army"—a merciless Taliban-like militia operating. They do not shrink from the use of firearms, robbery and theft with the confidence of a Robin Hood. The author clearly sympathises with the idea of violent revenge for unjust appropriation of property and ownership army. The thought of revenge is in all the novels quite strong. Therefore the vision of a village society, which peacefully transforms itself without any pressure from outside ("Chappar") is particularly remarkable.

Notes

1. Kapāṛiyā 1995: 3.
2. The modern Indian novel (coined "upanyās") started in Bengali, and particularly with Bankim Chandra Chattopadhyay (1838-1994).
3. "ākhir camārin-dhamārin hotā kis lie hai." (Kardam 1986:28)
4. Occasionally misspelled "Māyāpur" in my edition.

Bibliography

Kapâdiyâ 1995, Kapâdiyâ, Prem, *Mittî kî sauganḍh*. Naî dillî, 1995.

Kardam 1986, Kardam, Jayprakâú, *Karuṇâ: bauddh pṛṣṭhbhûmi par âdhârit upanyâs*. Gajiyâbâd, 1986.

Kardam 2003, Kardam, Jayprakâú, *Chappar (upanyâs)*. Dillî, 2003 (first 1994).

Satyaprakâú 1998, Satyaprakâú, *Jas tas bhaî saver*. Dillî, 1998.

2

Dalit Historiography: Poetry of Basudev Sunani

Saroj Mahananda

Introduction

Since 'narration' signifies a nation and narrative has traditionally been the main rhetorical device to discover what goes on inside people's heads and what it is like to live in a particular time, research in literature is not limited to mere appreciation of the artistic qualities in any given literature. It extends beyond the boundaries of the traditional format to engage itself with the questions of cultural representations, power, hegemony and justice. History is revisited with a new eye because today historiography is concerned not just about the rise and fall of empires or chronicling the events and episodes involving, or rather glorifying, the exploits of the power-that-be, but also about exploring the 'micro-history'[5] charting out the unknown or lesser known terrains of shared experience of people.

Case for Dalit History

There was a time when the concept of history was teleological. It meant that everything that took place was nothing but the handiwork of the Providence. But over the time humanism and the gradual secularisation of critical thoughts have influenced historiography. The 19th and 20th centuries saw the development of modern methods of historical investigation based on the use of primary source materials. Hegel introduced the concept of spirit (thesis, antithesis and synthesis), whereas Marx spoke of 'dialectical materialism' in relation to the history of the world. Process of nationalisation of history, as part of national revivals in 19th century, resulted with separation of "one's own" history from common universal history by a different way of perceiving, understanding and treating the past which constructed history as history of a nation.

Indian history being no exception, as an answer to the Euro-centric colonial history of India there was the Nationalist School of Historiography which reconstructed the past so as to suit the nationalist agenda. Riding the wave of nationalism India won Independence in 1947 with expectations galore. The fever of nationalism, however, had to give way to disillusionment among the people and by the 1980s there were enough problems in the nature of unemployment, peasant movements and insurgencies to be articulated by the Subaltern Studies group. The Subaltern School accused the Nationalist School of "elitism" which made the latter "unhistorical". In the words of Ranajit Guha:

> "What is clearly left out of this un-historical [elitist] historiography is the politics of the people. For parallel to the domain of elite politics there existed throughout the colonial period another domain of Indian politics in which the principal actors were not the dominant groups of the indigenous society or the colonial authorities but the subaltern classes and groups constituting the mass of the labouring population and intermediate strata in town and country—that is, the people. This was an autonomous domain, for, it neither originated from elite politics nor did its existence depend on the latter."[6]

Since its inception in 1982, this School very powerfully articulated and problematised the concept of Nation State, Civil Society, Power, Dominance, Subordination and Hegemony. In their attempt to 'write the history from below' both Marxists and Subaltern Studies groups had found a common platform. Needless to say that The Subaltern School took mighty pride in its kinship with the Marxist approach to the question of historiography as it substituted 'subaltern' for 'class' in its project to rectify the 'Nationalist' mistake. However, despite its pre-occupation with the concept of 'derivative discourse', 'indigenous community' and 'fragments'—and sporadic engagement by people like Guha in his essay "Chandra's Death[7]"— the Subaltern Studies group seems to have paid little attention to the 'micro-history' of the people.

By a curious stroke of fate, the *harijans/untouchables/dalits* of India find themselves with the Hindu community. They belong to Hinduism but Hinduism does not belong to them. Due to Sanskritisation most of them might have accepted the 'stories' of Hinduism but Hinduism is, far from accepting, least bothered about their 'stories' and most of which can be said to be constituting the 'micro-history' which has been missed by not only the colonial, nationalist, bourgeoisie, elitist historiography of India but also the Subaltern Studies groups[8]. One may consider this an oversight but this oversight is so clear that even Partha Chatterjee's *The Nation and its Fragments* (1993), which revels in the binaries of home and world, spiritual and material, woman and man, while considering the 'nation' and its 'fragments', maintains a steely silence about the powerful anti-caste movements associated with Phule, Periyar, or Ambedkar.[9] It is in this context Dalit writings in India assume tremendous significance. Neglected by Nationalists, Marxists and Subaltern Groups, the Dalits of India have no way but to write their own history.

Independent India has seen a flurry of literary and political activities by the Dalits. Being influenced by the writings of Ambedkar and Phule, quite a good number of Dalit writers and poets have been writing about their lives; they are trying to revive their lost identities through reconstruction and deconstruction. Autobiography has been a favourite genre for Dalit writers because they feel that only in the sphere of autobiography they can tell themselves and the world about their plight and predicaments. Debates about the authenticity of Dalit Writings have not discouraged them. Dalit writers from Maharastra, Karnataka, Tamil Nadu, Andhra Pradesh and Gujurat have remained in the forefront to document their lives, asserting their identities and challenging the hegemonic culture of Bramhanical society. Well known names in the field have been Om Prakash Valmiki (*Joothan*), Bama (*Kurukku*), Nam Dev Dhasal (*Golpitha*), Kumud Pawed ("The Story of My Sanskrit"), Sharan Kumar Limbale (*Akarmashi*), Laxman Mane (*Upara*) Sukhveer Singh ("Bayan-Bahar"), Gurudas Ram Alam ("To The Poet"), Nirav Patel ("Words"). The basis of Dalit writing is existential and experiential reality reflecting the oppressive hierarchy forced by Brahmanical purity/pollution logic. This reality is not limited to one or the other region but rather is a pan-Indian phenomenon. Through this perspective one can conceptualise the issue of Dalit identity which interrogates and reconstructs the boundaries of caste, sub-caste, language groups, region and the nation.

Dalit Writings in Odisha (Orissa)

Although, Odia dalit critics like Raj Kumar would prefer to trace the development of Odia Dalit Literature to 17th Century and consider other forms of protest literature as pioneers in this field. There was no distinct literary movement in the name of "Oriya Dalit Literature" during pre-independence era. Unlike Maharashtra, Gujarat, Karnataka, Andhra Pradesh and other Indian states Orissa has not experienced vigorous Dalit protest. It is only recently that some writers and poets have seriously started writing to represent "divided people".[10] The literary genres they have started experimenting which are limited to poetry, short stories, plays and critical essays. Novels, autobiographies and other forms of literature are rare. Among the story writers the name of "Ramachndra Sethi" finds prominence. In his stories, and particularly in "Dwitiya Buddha" (The Second Buddha), Sethi provides a powerful critique of the pervasive Jagannath Cult of Orissa. The untouchable protagonist, alter ego of the author, finds Sri Kshetra and Sri Jagannath in the body of his wife. Here both Jagannath, the sacred and the polluted untouchable body become metaphors to cross their swords on each other. Apparently there is no rejection of the Hindu God but the subtle suggestion is hardly missed. Among the poets who have been raising their voices powerfully against inequality and injustice are Bichitranand Nayak, Basudev Sunani, Kumaramani Tanti, Sanjay Bag, Anjubala Jena, Mohan Jena.

Works of Basudev Sunani

In this chapter, I would like to speak about the poems of Basudev Sunani who is a Veterinary Officer by profession but actually a versatile poet and writer writing passionately about Dalit life and cause. According to Odiya poet-translator, J.P. Das, "Primarily, Basudev Sunani is a poet who has refused to associate with the typical provincial, regional and pastoral literatures of Odisha". He presents through his poems a powerful critique of the so called mainstream but decadent, hypocritical, hegemonic Bramhanical culture and provides the alternative in the folk tradition and mythology typical to the dalits. An intense desire for a just and more human world marks the poetry of Sunani. He has to his credit several volumes of poetry with myriad colours of day to day life, all revolving round the humanistic concerns of the poet. Poems after poems deal with the touching issues of untouchability, questioning the very rational society which perpetrates such heinous crimes against humanity. Through his poems Sunani performs a twin function: annihilation of the hegemonic structure and reconstruction of the same on the foundation of humanity.

For instance, *Cast Out* (2008), is the name of the volume which is translated into English by J P. Das and contains powerful poems like "Coaching Center", "Body Purification", "Prayer", "Smell of Untouchability", "Nectar Seekers" and "Chelin Bai". In poems after poems Sunani very powerfully critiques the caste system of the country; his critiques range from simple questioning and expression of displeasure to the most complex process of myth making; for instance, in "Prayer" he puts a rhetorical question in the form of a challenge to God: Can God really differentiate between the surnames and return them to their respective holders if they are offered to Him in a bowl? It is pertinent to note that surnames are the indicators of caste and hierarchy in the society on the basis of which so much of oppression is legitimised. In "Coaching Center" he mocks at the sheer materialist agenda of the so called spiritual pursuits. But in the volumes titled *Asprushya (2001), and Chhi (2008),* one finds the formidable questions on the tradition and culture based on hypocrisy and inhumanity. The poem "Gothialen" which finds place in the volume *Chhi* is one of the most powerful poems and an exercise in myth-making which not only explores the already mentioned 'micro-history' of the Dalit community but also lays bare the corroding elements in the apparently invincible solid structure of the dominant culture. This poem narrates the moving story of a young dalit maiden who, in course of her duty as a cleaner/sweeper of the royal stable, had aroused the passion of the king and got pregnant. When her pregnancy could no longer be hidden due to bulging stomach, questions were asked about the identity of her lover. But, revealing the name of her lover made the whole royal establishment jittery; to save herself from the royal soldiers she tried to hide behind the horses inside the stable (*Goth*) but was killed because of the stampede caused by both men and the beasts. Since she died inside the stable she was made the deity of the 'Goth' (Gothialen) by her people and she is worshipped by some of the dalits even now. Transforming a victim of societal, sexual exploitation and violence into a deity, is a political act by the dalit community. Given their poverty stricken, dependent and subordinate position in the society they could not have made an effective protest; but certainly they have succeeded in writing their own history by commemorating her death. Effectively using the dramatic techniques of knocking and soliloquy Sunani presents before the readers the tragic predicament of a rape victim on the face of brutal force. Recurrent images of sensuality and violence work to lay bare the hypocrisy of the society.

On the other hand, there are Volumes titled *Mahula Bana* (1999), *Karadi Haat* (2005), and *Kalia Ubacha* (2011), where one finds all the more subtle but powerful satire on the dominant Oriya culture. In *Kalia Ubacha,* for example, one finds a sharp allusion to the origin and nature of the all powerful Jagannath Cult of Orissa. Sunani makes Kalia, another popular name for Lord Jagannath, the protagonist of this long poem. Kalia seems to have been fed up of the restrictive rituals of the Puri temple and goes to the sea beach in search of his childhood friend, a low caste person. He pours his heart out in front of His friend and expresses His shock, dismay and disillusionment at the way He has been appropriated by the dominant social groups. He fondly remembers His early days when He was the family deity of the Shabar Biswabasu (a tribal). He also feels cheated at the way the Kshyatriya King Indradyumna stole Him from Biswabasu. After hearing of the deities Indradyumna had appointed the cunning and crooked Bramhin Vidyapati to snare Lalita (the innocent daughter of Biswabasu) in amorous relation. Through Lalita Vidyapati got to know the secret place where the deities were worshipped and later on finding an opportune moment he stole the deities—Jagannath, Balabhadra and Subhadra—to hand them over to King Indradyumna. Alluding to the plight of the untouchables and non-Hindus who are not allowed to enter the Puri Temple and many other temples in Orissa, Kalia also expresses His strong displeasure at the way the Jagannath (literally, Lord of the Universe), has been made into Hindunath (Lord of the Hindus). Kalia feels suffocated at the hand of the priests and finds relief only in the company of His childhood friend who has nothing to offer, neither the wealth of the wealthy nor the knowledge and erudition of the Pandits but a compassionate heart of the dalit poet capable of human sympathy. Here in this poem as in many others, Sunani works in the realm of the folk and creates a parallel history of his people.

Thus, Sunani's works constitute not only documentation of the folk life, history, music and an alternate belief system but also provides a powerful alternative to the dominant Bramhanical structure.

Notes

1. Carlo Ginzburg and Natalie Zemon Davis pioneered the genre of historical writing known as "micro-history" which attempted to understand the mentalities and decisions of individuals—mostly peasants—within their limited milieu using contracts, court documents and oral histories.
2. Ranajit Guha, "Introduction" *A Subaltern Studies Reader,* New Delhi, OUP, 2003 (1997), pp. xiv-xv.
3. In this moving study of death (through enforced abortion after an illicit affair) of a low caste woman Guha not only unravels the 'community' but also the conflict, the brutal exploitation, the power relation which is 'sited at a depth within the indigenous society, well beyond the reach of the disciplinary arm of the State'. According to Guha all these dimensions are often concealed through a blending of 'indigenous feudal ideology…with colonial anthropology." Sumit Sarkar, *Writing Social History*, New Delhi, OUP, 2011 (1997), pp. 93-94.
4. This line of argument is anticipated by Kancha Ilaih in the introduction to his essay when he says that the *Subaltern Studies* is no exception to the unambiguous neglect of Mainstream Historiography . "Productive Labour, Consciousness and History: The Dalitbahujan Alternative". *Subaltern Studies IX.* Eds. Shahid Amin and Dipesh Chakrabarty, New Delhi, OUP, 2005 (1996), p. 165
5. Sumit Sarkar, *Writing Social History*, New Delhi, OUP, 2011 (1997), p. 96.
6. There are at least ninety-three Scheduled Caste communities in Orissa having different customs, traditions, dialects and deities of their own. It is in this sense Dalits in Orissa, as elsewhere, are divided communities.

Bibliography

Primary Sources

Sunani, Basudev. *Asprushya*. Nuapada (Odisha, India): Ishaan - Ankit Prakashani, 2007 (2001).

Sunani, Basudev. *Cast Out; Poems of Anger and Angst.* Trans. J.P. Das. Bhubaneswar (India): Rupantar, 2008.

Sunani, Basudev. *Chhee*. Bhubaneswar (Odisha,India): Time Pass, 2008.

Sunani, Basudev. *Dalit Encounter*. Ed. Jagdish Lal. Sangrur (Punjab): MNKY Prakashan, 2009.

Sunani, Basudev. *Dalit Sanskritir Itihas*. Nuapada (Odisha,India): Ishaan - Ankit Prakashani, 2009.

Sunani, Basudev. Kalia Ubaacha. Bhubaneswar (Odisha, India): Sahitya ShwetaPadma, 2011.

Sunani, Basudev. *Karadi Haat*. Nuapada (Odisha, India): Ishaan - Ankit Prakashani, 2005.

Secondary Sources

Basnett, Susan and A. Lefevere. *Constructing Cultures: Essays on Literary Translation*. Clevedon: Multilingual Matters, 1998.

Basnett, Susan and A. *Translation Studies*. 3rd Edition. London: Routledge, 2002.

Basnett, Susan and A. eds. *Translation, History and Culture*. London: Pinter, 1990.

Bhabha, Homi K. "Introduction: Narrating the Nation". *Nation and Narration*. Ed. Homi K. Bhabha. London: Routledge, 1991 (1990).

Bhabha, Homi K. *The Location of Culture: Discussing Post Colonial Culture*. London: Routledge, 1996.

Bhoi, Bhima. *Stuti Chintamani*. Cuttack: Dharma Grantha Store, 1992.

Chedwankar, Prahlad. "Empty Advice". *An Anthology of Dalit Literature*, Eds. Mulk Raj Anand and Eleanor Zealot. New Delhi: Gyan Publishing House, 1992.

Chatterjee, Partha. "Caste and Subaltern Consciousness." *Subaltern Studies VI*. Ed. Ranajit Guha. New Delhi: OUP, 2005 (1989).

Chatterjee, Partha. *Nationalist Thought and the Colonial World: a Derivative Discourse?* Minneapolis (MN): University of Minnesota Press, 1993.

Chatterjee, Partha. *Nation and its Fragments: Colonial and Post Colonial Histories*. Princeton, NJ: Princeton UP, 1993.

Cohn, Bernard S. "The Command of Language and the Language of Command." *Subaltern Studies IV*. Ed. Ranajit Guha. New Delhi: OUP, 2005 (1985).

Dangle, Arjun, ed. *Poisoned Bread: Translation from Modern Marathi Dalit Literature.* Hyderabad: Orient Longman, 1992.

Das, Chittaranjan. *A Glimpse into Oriya Literature*. Bhubaneswar: Oriya Sahitya Academi, 1982.

Freeman, James M. *Untouchable: History of an Indian Life*. London: George Allen and Unwin, 1978.

Gramsci,Antonio. *Selections from the prison notebooks*. Hyderabad: Orient Longman Limited, 1996.

Guha, Ranajit. "Dominance without Hegemony and Its Historiography." *Subaltern Studies VI*. Ed. Ranajit Guha. New Delhi: OUP, 2005 (1989).

Guha, Ranajit. Ed. *A Subaltern Studies Reader*. New Delhi: Oxford University Press, 2003 (1997).

Hardtmann, Eva-Maria. *The Dalit Movement in India*. New Delhi: OUP, 2009.

Illaih, Kancha. "Productive Labour, Consciousness and History: The Dalit Bahujan Alternative."

Subaltern Studies IX. Shahid Amin and Dipesh Chakravarty eds. New Delhi: OUP, 2005 (1996).

Khare, R.S. Ed. *Caste, Hierarchy and Individualism*. 2nd edition. New Delhi: OUP, 2006.

Mallik, Basanta Kumar. *Paradigms of Dissent and Protest: Social Movements in Eastern India* New Delhi: Manohar, 2004.

Nayak, Bichitrananda. *Mukti Anirbana*. Cuttack: Cuttack Students' Store, 1993.

Niranjana, Tejashwini. *Siting Translation. History, Post-Structuralism and the ColonialContext*. Berkley, Los Angeles: University of California Press. 1992.

Omvedt, Gail. *Dalits and the Democratic Revolution: Dr Ambedkar and the Dalit Movement in Colonial India*. New Delhi: Penguin, 1994.

Pradhan, Atul Chandra. *The Nationalist Movement*. New Delhi: Amar Prakash, 1993.

Preston, James J. "Goddess Temples in Orissa: An anthropological survey". *Religion in Modern India*. Ed. Giri Raj Gupta. New Delhi: Vikas Publishing House, 1983.

Rao, Y. C. *Writing Dalit History and Other Essays*. New Delhi: Kanishka Publishers, 2007.

Roy, B.C. *Orissa under the Mughals*. Calcutta: Punthi Pustak, 1981.

Sarkar, Sumit. *Writing Social History*. New Delhi: OUP, 2011 (1997).

Spivak, Gayatri C. "Can the Subaltern Speak?" *Marxism and the Interpretation of Culture*. Eds. Cary Nelson and Lawrence Grossberg. 1998.

Spivak, Gayatri C. "Subaltern Studies: Deconstructing Historiography". *Subaltern Studies IV* Ed. Ranajit Guha. New Delhi: OUP, 2005 (1985).

Said, Edward. *Culture and Imperialism*. New York: Vintage Books,1994.

Said, Edward. *Nationalism, Colonialism and Literature*. Derry, Ireland: Field Day, 1988.

Said, Edward. *Orientalism*. London: Penguin Books, 1978.

Sethi, Rama Chandra. "Dwitiya Buddha". *Rama Charita Manasa*. Banapur (Orissa): Punyasloka Prakashani, 1980.

St-Pierre, Paul and P. C. Kar. Eds. *In Translation; Reflections, Refractions, Transformations.* Delhi: Pencraft International, 2005.

Trivedi, Harish. "The Politics of Post-Colonial Translation". *Translation: its Theory and Practice.* Ed. A.K. Singh. New Delhi: Creative Books, 1996.

Williams, Raymond. *Marxism and Literature*. London: Oxford University Press, 1997.

Young, Robert. *White Mythologies: Writing History and the West*. London: Routledge, 1990.

Young, Robert. *Colonial Desire: Hybridity in Theory, Culture and Race*. London: Routledge, 1995.

Journals/E-Sources

Barik, Radhakanta. "Dalit Itihasa Tatwa". *Bikalpa Bichara*, July-Sept, Bargarh (Orissa), 1994.

Kumar, Ràj. "Oriya Dalit literature: A Historical Perspective". *The Fourth World: Journal of the Marginalised People*. Oct. No. 2. Bhubaneswar (Orissa): NISWASS, 1995.

Lears, T. J. Jackson. "The Concept of Cultural Hegemony: Problems and Possibilities." The American Historical Review, Vol. 90. No. 3 (Jun. 1985), pp. 567-593. http://www.jstor.org.stable/1860957

Pattanayak, D.P. "Aryanisation of Orissa". *Orissa Historical Research Journal*, Vol. 7, No. 1. 1956.

Punalekar, S.P. "Experience, Perceptions and Reality: A Study of Dalit literature in Maharashtra". *Collection of Unpublished Seminar Papers*. Surat: Centre for Social Studies, 1988.

Srivastava, Vivek Kumar. "Pandit Nehru and his View of History", *Mainstream*, Vol. XLIX, No. 48, November 19, 2011.

3

Construction of Dalit Identity: The Alternative Socio-Cultural Movements in Tamil Nadu, Kerala and Andhra Pradesh

Bolleddu Siva Nagaiah

There has been a long tradition of intellectual reconstruction of the Dalit identity in India. The eminent activists who contributed to the process include Phule, Periyar and Ambedkar, among others. Before them, the *Bakti* saints made a remarkable contribution in the form of questioning the Brahmanical hegemony. They questioned the religious restrictions on worship during the 10th and 13th centuries, because of which the Bakti movement became popular among the *sudras* and *ati-shudras*. Later, during the Colonial period and postcolonial period to some extent, the construction of Dalit identity took the greater momentum and it was due the practicable understanding of the Indian society by non-brahman thinkers and activists who had seen India through their socio-political lens. The pioneers of such great non-branman movments in the Adi-movements are found in every part of India but their contribution in awakening India from socio-political point of view is not historicised properly. The paper explores the contribution of the Adi-movements, the non-Brahman movements against the Brahmin hegemony from the South and how they contributed for the intellectual re-construction of the Dalit identity and the identity movements in the contemporary period leading to the culmination of the reconstruction of the Dalit identity.

I

To begin with, Panditha Iyothee Thass (1845–1914) was a Dalit philosopher who campaigned for education among the untouchables. Iyothee Thass, an emancipatory Buddhist hailed form Tamil Nadu, known for his struggle against the social irrationalities of valorised casteism and religionism. Iyothee Thass re-discovered the original casteless Tamil and Dravidian identity and Buddhist identity by re-interpreting the subcontinent's religio-cultural history. Ravi Kumar, a Dalit Activist and founder of Navayana publications records that Iyothee Thass gained expertise in Tamil literature, philosophy, Siddha and had good knowledge of English, Sanskrit and Pali… He established the *Advaidananda Sabha* in 1876 and launched a magazine called Dravida Pandian along with Rev. John Rathinam in 1885. He issued a statement in 1886 announcing that the so-called untouchables' are not Hindus. He established the *Dravida Mahajana Sabha* in 1891 and during the very first Census urged the so-called untouchables to register themselves as casteless Dravidians. This in fact makes Tamil Dalits the true descendents of the anti-Brahmin legacy which is today claimed by non-Brahmin and non-Dalits.[11]

However the rich and determined contribution by Iyothee Thass through his writings in awaking the Dalit masses needs re-interpretation from contemporary socio-political, cultural point of view. Iyothee Thas set up several schools for Dalits and his writings are remarkably modern for espousing the cause of social emancipating, Buddhism, rationalism and the new egalitarian Dravidian identity.[12] He considered the Brahmins mentally, morally and culturally depressed as they clanged on to anachronistic beliefs and obscurantist practices. Ravi Kumar writes, "Thass launched a weekly called 'Tamilan' in 1907 and published it till his demise in 1914. Here, he devoted his energies in critiquing the Swarajya politics of the Congress. Thass was the driving force behind the establishment of several panchama schools in Chennai. He focused on education and the land issue. He interpreted Indian history in an entirely different light in the work Indirar Desa Sarithiram (History of India) which can be classified as subaltern history in a true sense."[13]

Another prominent socio-political moment in Tamil Nadu was led by E.V.Rama Swamy (1879-1973) popularly known as Periyar. Periyar led the self-respect movement in Tamil Nadu and it was considered as one of the greatest anti-Brahman movements in India. The self-respect movement, lead by Periyar targeted the Brahmin dominance, criticising the idol worship. Aloysius comments on Periyar: His focus was not God and religion in general or in the philosophical sense but religion in particular – the Brahminical religion – taken in its practical – social dimension of buttressing up social iniquity and in humanity."[14]

All the religions, being historical creations, tend to accumulate beliefs and practices that become anachronistic and anti-social. Periyar clarifies that:

"The self-respect movement was started with the objective of instilling a sense of self-respect in the people of this country and to unify them. The self-respect movement really endeavors in transparency, to explain why and how the people of our country had lost their self-pride, to assert that the obstacles in their way should be abolished and indeed to abolish such obstacles".[15]

Periyar educated the Dravidians and Adi-Dravidians to bring about a cultural revolt with an aim of making society casteless and egalitarian. Braj Ranjan Mani observes:

Stressing egalitarian social relations across caste, community and gender lines, Periyar advocated the overthrow of caste and instituted non-Brahmanic forms of marriage celebrating the equality of women and her right to choose life-partner and other such practices designed to give a death blow to the Brahmanical order. Presenting a radical critique of the religious beliefs and practices in a variety of ways, Periyar wanted to demolish the whole Brahmanic structure of society which he saw as the root cause of the degradation and sub-ordination of Women and the non-brahman populace.[16]

Periyar joined the congress in 1919 and became a prominent figure in Tamil Congress. But soon he saw it a Brahman Tamil Congress and left it to organise the self-respect movement. Periyar also disagreed with Gandhi on issues like caste, culture and nationalism.

II

Another significant movement of Dalit identity took place in Kerala. The movements led by Ayyankali, Pokayil Yohannan and Pamapady John Joseph had a polemical role to enlighten the Dalits of Kerala. Sri Narayana Guru (1856-1928) was an active socio-political and religious reformer for nearly four decades during the most critical period of Kerala's history. He believed in the message of 'one god, one religion and one caste,' which developed a new consciousness among the Dalits. The backward caste movements in Kerala differed from other movements like that of Jotirao Phule, whose movement consisted of Shudras and ati-Shudras (the untouchable) and women. But such an attempt was absent in Kerala and the movement lead by Sree Narayana Guru remained mostly the movement for the upliftment and empowerment of the Izhavas.

Among the Dalit movements in Kerala, the movement by Ayyankali was of great success in constructing Dalit identity. Ayyankali, an illiterate Dalit, unlike Sree Narayana Guru, was not philosophical. His movement was humanistic and democratic. To him, socio-cultural issues were more important than the economic issues. Ayyankali fought for the rights of his people to use public space and for education. By doing so, Ayyankali successfully contributed to the formation of the individual identity.

Ayyankali established open school in Vengannoor in 1904 but faced severe resistance from the high caste Hindus. He gathered the scheduled castes to go on strike and continued it for one full year. To protect the strikers against criminal elements recruited by landlords, a small group of youth known as "Ayyankali Pada" was formed under his organisation. Another element that Ayyankali movement concentrated on was performing folk arts. Ayyankali collected small band of youth belonging to his caste and trained them in martial and folk arts like 'Pattukachery', 'Parijakali', 'Kolkali', Kurathiattom', Kakkarassi drama' and 'Valli drama.' This was his first attempt at identity construction.

Formation of 'Sadhu Jana Paripalana Sangam' (SJPS) was another significant form of identity formation in the Ayyankali movement. It was democratic in character and gender sensitive. Kerala Pulayar Maha Sabha by T.T. Kesava Shashtri, son-in-law of Ayyankali, obtained the four basic rights for the Dalits: right to appear in public places decently dressed, right to education, cultural rights and the right to be represented in the government. These were the subtle forms of the assertion of the Dalit identity.

III

The Dalit movements and literature in Andhra Pradesh began as early as 1900. The Adi-Hindu movements in Hyderabad and Adi-Dravida movement in Andhra region played significant roles in constructing the Dalit identity in the pre-independence period. The Adi-Hindu movement under Nizam rule was led by Bagya Reddy Varma (1888-1939), who organised 'Jagan Mitra Mandali' in 1906, found 'Manya Samngam' in 1911 and the Adi-Hindu organisation in the same year. Bagya Reddy Varma and his followers strongly fought for the compulsory education to the Dalit children and severely opposed the practices like child marriages, eating meet and using drink in marriages and also against the uncivic notions like 'Jogini', Murti' and 'Basivi' through which young and uneducated untouchable girls were devoted to gods and goddesses. Between 1906 and 1916, Bagya Reddy Varma's concentration was particularly on educating Dalits through folk songs and street plays. He went across the entire Telangana region and gave the message of revolution to the Dalits. Ariga Ramaswami and B. Syam Sundhar were other contemporaries of Bagya Reddy Varma who contributed to the construction of Dalit identity in Hyderabad state.

The Adi-Andhra Movement took place in the coastal parts of Andhra Pradesh in the Madras Presidency. The common interface between the Adi-Hindu movement in Hyderabad and the Adi-Andhra Movement in Andhra was that both the movements were led by Bagya Reddy Varma in both the regions. The Adi-Andhra movement took place in 1917 with the 'First *Provincial Panchama Mahajana Sabha*' organised in Vijayawada. Bagya Reddy Varma opposed the use of the term *panchamas.* Some of the significant resolutions were: providing education to Dalit children, forming separate schools for Dalit children, allowing Dalits to use government wells, schools and public shelter, among others. The Adi-Andhra Conferences were held every year.[17]

The rise of Adi-Andhra movement became a suitable occasion for political mobilisation. Dalit writers like Boyi Bhimanna, Kusuma Dharmmanna and Jala Rangaswamy wrote against caste oppression, untouchability and discrimination stressing that that the Dalits were the original inhabitants of the Telugu region. Gurram Jashuva's *Piradousi* (1932), *Gabbilam* (The Bat); Kusuma Dharmanna's *Nalla Dhoratham* (1933), *Harijana Chathakam* (1933), *Madhyapana Nishedham* (1930); Boyi Bhimanna's *Paleru* (1940), *Cooliraju* (1947) and *Jana Padhuni Jabhulu* (1940); Jala Rangaswami's *Mala Shuddi* (1930); Nakka China Venkataiah's *Harijana Keerthanalu* (1935); Nuthakki Abraham and Premaiah were among those written and remained instrumental in constructing the Dalit identity from Telugu land.

IV

A scrupulous study of the above discussed movements makes us understand that the socio-cultural movements lead by the Dalit philosophers from the three states have a common goal that is nothing but to pave the way for an alternative society. In their view an alternative society is possible only by deconstructing the dominance of Brahmanism on one hand and reconstructing the Dalit identity on the other so as to bring the forbidden, unrecorded and excluded Dalit cultural aesthetics as an integral part to be identified with self-respect and pride in the mainstream society for which they struggled all the way. Their writings remained an evidence and will help the coming generation of Dalits to retrieve the lost identity with a sense of self-assertion and gender empowerment.

Notes and References

1. Ravi Kumar, Iyothee Thass: The Politics of Naming, *Countercurrents. Org*. Web. Sept., 2005. <http://www.countercurrents.org/dalit-ravikumar280905.htm>.
2. Braj Ranjan Mani, *Debrahmanising History: Dominance and Resistance in Indian Society,* New Delhi: Manohar, 2007, 314, Print.
3. Ravi Kumar, Iyothee Thass: The Politics of Naming, *Countercurrents. Org*. Web. Sept., 2005. <http://www.countercurrents.org/dalit-ravikumar280905.htm>.
4. Aloysius, G, *Periyar on Islam*, New Delhi: Critical Quest, 2004, 4, Print.
5. Aloysius, G., 5.
6. Braj Ranjan Mani, pp. 324-25.
7. Gail Omvedt, *Dalits and Democratic Revolution: Dr Ambedkar and the Dalit Movement in Colonial India,* New Delhi: Sage, 1994, 118, Print.

4

The Plight of Dalit Women in Contemporary Indian Society

Siddaramu, B.

The impact of caste system on the educational, social, and economical status of Dalit women still exists in contemporary India. Hinduism has degraded Dalit women beyond imagination. The situation of Dalit women in India is just unexplainable. They are one among the worst sufferers of socio-cultural, political and economic exploitation, injustice, oppression and violence. Their woes and miseries are boundless. They are the ones who form 'real' teeming millions in India, and are affected by all kinds of social and economic oppressions. They are mainly employed in unorganised sector of the Indian economy as daily wagers and marginal workers. The lack of adequate employment opportunities, limited skills and illiteracy have made their mobility extremely limited and prevent them from achieving independent status. This paper highlight the harsh reality of the suppression, struggle and torture Dalit women face every day of their miserable lives. Dr B.R. Ambedkar, an architect of the Indian constitution, makes it very clear in his article titled "The rise and fall of Hindu woman" that the root cause of suffering for women in India are these so called Hindu religious books. He pointed out that the laws of Manu on the status of women are very important in moulding the Hindu attitude and perspective (Indian perspective) towards women, perpetuated and maintained through Hindu personal laws based on shastras, caste and endogamy, i.e., the base of Indian patriarchy. He attacked *Manusmriti* as a major source, which legitimises the denial of freedom, self-respect, right to education, property, divorce, etc., to women by attributing a very lofty ideal to them. This article makes an attempt to explain the plight of Dalit women in contemporary India.

One cannot understand India without understanding the complete nature and scope of the caste system in Indian life. Caste considerations dominate people's lives from birth to death. This understanding of the caste system and how it controls and regulates social, economic, political and religious life is absolutely essential to interpreting the Indian reality. India is not a homogenous society where there is a level playing field on which everyone can prosper. Caste continues to dominate Indian society. The caste system is truly a crippling disease to approximately 250 million Dalits in India today (Narula, 1999). The impact of caste system on the educational, social, and economical status of Dalit women still exists in contemporary India. Hinduism has degraded Dalit women beyond imagination. The situation of Dalit women in India is just unexplainable. They are one among the worst sufferers of socio-cultural, political and economic exploitation, injustice, oppression and violence. Their woes and miseries are boundless. They are the ones who form 'real' teeming millions in India, and are affected by all kinds of social and economic oppressions. They are mainly employed in unorganised sector of the Indian economy as daily wagers and marginal workers. The lack of adequate employment opportunities, limited skills and illiteracy have made their mobility extremely limited and prevent them from achieving independent status. This paper highlights the harsh reality of the suppression, struggle and torture Dalit women face every day of their miserable lives.

The hardships of Dalit women are not simply due to their poverty, economical status, or lack of education, but are a direct result of the severe exploitation and suppression by the upper classes, which is legitimised by Hindu religious scriptures (Thind, Agarwal, 1999).

Dr B.R. Ambedkar, an architect of the Indian constitution, makes it very clear in his article titled "The rise and fall of Hindu woman" that the root cause of suffering for women in India are these so called Hindu religious books. He pointed out that the laws of Manu on the status of women are very important in moulding the Hindu attitude and perspective (Indian perspective) towards women, perpetuated and maintained through Hindu personal laws based on shastras, caste and endogamy, i.e. the base of Indian patriarchy. He attacked Manusmriti as a major source, which legitimises the denial of freedom, self-respect, right to education, property, divorce etc., to women by attributing a very lofty ideal to them. He observes in the law book of Manu that the killing of a woman is like the drinking of liquor, a minor offence. When he was in Colombia University, he wrote to a friend on the need to educate the depressed classes, especially the womenfolk. To quote him: "We shall see better days soon and our progress will be greatly accelerated if male education is pursued side by side with female education". (Mathew, 1991:74). Ambedkar perceived education as a catalyst for a movement for self-respect and self-help.

Ambedkar's defense for women as the Law Minister of free India appeared in the form of the Hindu Code Bill in Parliament on 11th April 1947, which invited strong opposition from the Hindu orthodoxy in post-independent India. The Bill provided for several basic rights to women. It sought to abolish different marriage systems prevalent among Hindus and to establish monogamy as the only legal system. It aimed at conferment of right to property and adoption of women. It provided for restitution of conjugal rights and judicial separation. It attempted to unify the Hindu code in tune with progressive and modern thought. (Mathew, 1991:73-73; Ahir, 1990).

In 1948, when the Hindu Code Bill was introduced in parliament and debated on the floor of the house, the opposition was strong against the Bill. Ambedkar tried his level best to defend the Bill by pointing out the drawbacks of Indian society and arguing that the ideals in the Bill are based on the Constitutional principles of equality, liberty and fraternity and that in the Indian society characterised by the caste system and the oppression of women since women are deprived of equality, a legal frame work is necessary for a social change in which women have equal rights with men. He also pointed out that the aim of the Bill was "to codify the rules of Hindu Law which are scattered in innumerable decisions of High Courts and of the Privy Council which form a bewildering motley to the common man". (Arya, 2000:63). However, the Bill could not withstand the opposition from the Hindu orthodoxy. Their major argument was that the Bill was an attempt at the "demolition of the entire structure and fabric of Hindu Society. The very foundations not only of one pillar but of all the pillars on which the Hindu society rests are shaken". In reality, the Bill was a threat to patriarchy on which traditional family structure, was bounded and that was the major reason behind the opposition. Therefore, on the eve of the first elections in 1951 Prime Minister Jawaharlal Nehru dropped the Bill by saying that there was too much opposition. On this issue, the then Law Minister Dr Ambedkar resigned. Books like the Manusmriti divide people into a stratified caste system and promote inequality between men and women (Thind; Agarwal). According to the *Manusmriti*, women have no right to education, independence, or wealth. It not only justifies the treatment of dalit women as a sex object and promotes child marriage, but also justifies a number of violent atrocities on women (Agarwal, 1999).

The situation of Dalit women in India is just unexplainable. They are one among the worst sufferers of socio-cultural, political and economic exploitation, injustice, oppression and violence. Their woes and miseries are boundless. They are the ones who form 'real' teeming millions in India, and are affected by all kinds of social and economic oppressions. They are mainly employed in unorganised sector of the Indian economy as daily wagers and marginal workers. The lack of adequate employment opportunities, limited skills and illiteracy have made their mobility extremely limited and prevent them from achieving independent status.

According to the National Commission for Scheduled Castes and Scheduled Tribes 2000, approximately 75 per cent of the Dalit girls drop out of primary school despite the strict laws of the Government of India, which hold reservations for Dalit children (*National Commission*). The majority of the stories we read and hear are of bright young Dalit girls who are punished by the upper caste teachers in rural area of India, for daring to score good grades. According to the "National Commission for Scheduled Castes and Scheduled Tribes", the majority of the educated people are of the upper caste, many of which may practice caste-based discrimination. Therefore, Dalit girls feel discouraged to enter education and we see the lowest literacy rate for Dalit girls compared to the total population of educated upper caste girls (*National Commission)*. The Annual Report of University Grant Commision for 1999-2000, shows that Dalits in general have very low participation rates in higher education (*Annual Reports of University)*.

Since only a small percentage of the total population of Dalit women are educated, the fate of the majority is very grim. According to India's Ministry of Labour, 85 per cent of the Dalit women have the most formidable occupations and work as agricultural labourers, scavengers, sweepers, and disposers of human waste. Many of these women work for minimal wages under the upper caste landlords, since it is proposed that by the National Commission for SC/ST that 85 per cent of the Dalits are landless (*News Archives*). When the Dalit women refuse to work for ridiculously low wages or fail to follow their harsh orders it results in open violence, humiliation, beatings, rape, and jail. There are also a number of cases where the houses of Dalit women have been burnt down (Agarwal).

Violence against women in India has never been uncommon phenomenon. Women in the Indian society have been victims of humiliation, torture and harassment as long as one can observe from written records and newspaper reports. Dalit women have been the object of violence in greater degree from higher caste men. They have been subjected to rape, molestation, kidnapping, abduction, homicide, physical and mental torture, immoral traffic and sexual abuse. There is a tendency of increase in the cases of violence against Dalit women. According to the National Crime Statistics (India:2001) there were 2,824 reported cases of rape, 4,591 cases of serious injuries, 517 cases of murder, 2,261 cases of kidnapping and abduction, 8,527 cases of physical torture, 10,425 cases of eve-teasing, 3,588 cases of molestation and sexual harassment, 556 cases of importation of girls, and 4,452 cases under Immoral Tariff Act. Thus, there were 37,841 registered cases of violence against Dalit Women in the year 2001 alone (India: 2001). It should be noted that in India about 90 per cent crimes against Dalit women are not reported to the police for the fear of social ostracism and threat to personal safety and security. Also the legal proceedings are so complicated, tardy, time consuming, costly and unfriendly to Dalits that usually they do not approach courts or other law enforcing agencies for their redressal. Besides, a huge number of Dalit women are dragged in the profession of flesh-trade and prostitution. Many of these unfortunate women are minor and innocent girls who are lured by unscrupulous touts and agents into this profession. The religious practices like *Devadashi* and *Sevikas* of the temples in south and western India also force them into this profession and are given religious colour.

Dalit women are often employed in agricultural farms owned by higher caste feudal landlords during tilling, sowing, irrigating, cutting and harvesting seasons, and are on their mercy for their bread and butter. They are always paid far less wages than prescribed by the rules and have to work for longer hours. During the course of their work in the fields they are often sexually exploited by their feudal landlords. They are hardly able to resist routine kind of the maltreatment and misbehaviour meted out to them. Not only that, many of them are kept as bonded labourers by their landlords and are not paid their legitimate wages at all. In such cases, they are given only some food and cloths. They do not even know how to seek legal help and redressal to overcome their bonded status. There are several schemes of upliftment of Dalit women by the State and the Central Governments. But, the benefits of such schemes and programmes rarely reach to them. Indian bureaucracy is hopelessly insensitive, inefficient and corrupt. It hardly cares for them and their plights. Whatever funds come for their improvement, are cornered by unscrupulous local politicians, government functionaries and petty bureaucrats. Thus, the funds which are earmarked by the government for their welfare, are hardly able to bring any noticeable change in their life. They remain hapless, ignorant, exploited and oppressed. They are the victims of worst kind of patriarchy, feudalism, casteism, corruption and insentivity of the Indian society. Their plights are endless, life is difficult and full of miseries (Rajendra Prasad Jaiswal).

For the majority of Dalit women, the panchayat election process masks strong, caste-based patriarchal control over them and the enjoyment of their rights. Around 85 per cent of Dalit women were pushed into panchayat politics primarily by dominant castes or their husbands, the former often working through the women's husbands. Dominant castes also for the most part sought to directly engineer elections by consensus, thereby making the reservation policy redundant. The primary tool for this, and the most significant factor drawn from the research, was *benami* or proxy politics. The effective use of proxy candidature provided legitimised political space for primarily dominant caste men and secondarily Dalit men to exploit Dalit women, and reinforce their own interests and the suppression of these women. At the same time, this denied Dalit women's right to independent and empowered participation in local governance. To ensure success in proxy politics, various strategies were employed drawing on Dalit women's vulnerabilities: their low gender status in the family (as economically dependent and bounded within marital and kinship relations); their low gender, caste and class status (as woman and Dalit, as illiterate and labourer) in society; their old age or widowhood status; exploiting and deepening intra-Dalit divisions through supporting one sub-caste against another, often to prevent a more assertive or vocal sub-caste member from being elected. Livelihood dependency and lack of sufficient financial resources to meet election expenses also made the women vulnerable to proxy politics especially from dominant castes and political parties (dominated by dominant caste).

Once elected dominant caste male, control over panchayat resources and ingrained discriminatory attitudes continued to govern to a large extent the experiences of Dalit women panchayat representatives. At least three-quarters of these women were either proxies or faced strong opposition and obstructions while attempting to work for the benefit of their community. Around one-third of women are able to freely and independently exercise their right to political participation against tremendous odds, the majority are made to effectively act as proxies for primarily dominant caste men. Most elected Dalit women feel they are treated differently from other local government representatives primarily due to being female and Dalit. Overt discriminatory practices are prevalent in local government offices, including prohibitions on Dalit women sitting on chairs alongside other elected representatives; drinking water or tea from vessels used by dominant caste elected representatives. Some Dalit women attempt to actively participate in meetings and taking decisions, but are silenced or ignored; subjected to 'no confidence' motions to remove them from office; denied information and support to undertake their duties; etc. This situation is not helped where government officials refuse to address caste and gender discrimination or proxy representation as part of their monitoring local government functioning. (Jayshree Mangubhai, Aloysius Irudayam, Emma Sydenham, 2009).

The Committee on the Elimination of Racial Discrimination on the Indian Government's Report in 2007 noted its concern over the under representation of Dalits in all levels of government. "Dalit candidates, especially women, are frequently forcibly prevented from standing for election or, if elected, forced to resign from village councils or other elected bodies or not to exercise their mandate, [and] that many Dalits are not included in electoral rolls or otherwise denied the right to vote..."

Dalit women of India have been living in the culture of silence throughout the centuries. They do not have any control over their own bodies, earnings, and lives. The extreme expression of violence, exploitation and oppression against them is visible in forms of hunger, malnutrition, disease, physical and mental torture, rape, illiteracy, ill-health, unemployment, insecurity and inhuman treatment. The collective forces of feudalism, casteism, and patriarchy have made their lives just a hell. Thus, it is being felt that sincere and honest efforts for the improvement in Dalit women's status are urgently required.

References

Agarwal, S. 1999. *Genocide of women in Hinduism*. Sudrastan Books. Jabalpur. India.

Ahir, D.C. (1990), *The Legacy of Ambedkar,* Delhi.

Ahuja, Ram (2003), *Social Problems in India,* Rawat, Jaipur.

Ambedkar, B.R. "*Women and Counter Revolution", "Riddles of Hindu Women" in Dr Baba Saheb Ambedkar: Writings and Speeches,* Vol.3, Department of Education, Government of Maharashtra, 1987.

Chandra Ramesh, Mitra Sangh (2003). *Dalit Identity in the New Millennium,* Commonwealth, New Delhi.

Government of India, Government off (2005). *Census of India (2001),* Registrar General and Census Commissioner of India, New Delhi.

Haksar, Nandita, (1986) *Demystification of Law for Women*, Lancer Press, New Delhi.

Heywood, Andrew, (1998) *Political Ideologies: An Introduction*, Macmillan Press, London.

India, Government of (2001). *Crime in India,* National Crime Record Bureau, New Delhi.

Issacs, Harold R. (1965), *India's Ex-untouchables,* John Day, New York.

Jayshree Mangubhai, Aloysius Irudayam, Emma Sydenham (2009*), Dalit Women's Right to Political Participation in Rural Panchayati Raj: A Study of Gujarat and Tamil Nadu*, Published by IDEAS.

Limaye, Champa (1999) Women: Power and Progress, B.R.Publishing Corporation, New Delhi.

Mahar, J. Michael (1998). *The Untouchables in Contemporary India*, Rawat, Jaipur.

Manu (1920). *Manu Smriti: The laws of Manu with the Bhasya of Medhatithi*. Translated by Ganga Natha Jha. University of Calcutta, Calcutta, India.

Mathew, Thomas (1991). *Ambedkar: Reform or Revolution*, Segment Books, New Delhi.

Narula. S. (1999). *Broken People: Caste Violence Against India's "Untouchables"* London: Human Rights Watch.

Rajendra Prasad Jaiswal. *Plight of Rural Dalit Women in India: A Sociological Analysis* Mahatma Gandhi Kashi Vidyapith, India.

Rege, Shamila (ed.) (2003). *"Sociology of Gender: Challenges of Feminist Sociological Knowledge"* in S. Rege (ed.) Themes in Indian Sociology, Vol. 1, Sage, New Delhi.

Roy Burman, B.K. (1977). *The Problems of Untouchables* in Romesh Thaper (ed.) *Tribe, Caste and Religion in India,* McMillan, New Delhi.

Sonia Mahey. *The Status of Dalit Women in India's Caste Based System,* University of Alberta.

The National Commission for Scheduled Castes and Scheduled Tribes, Government of India.

The Annual Reports of University Grant Commision, Government of India.

Thind, G.S. *Our Indian Sub-Continent Heritage*. Crosstown Press, LTD. British Columbia, Canada.

Verma, J.M.S. (ed.) (1999). *Gender Justice in India*, Spellbound, Rohtak.

Usha K.B. (2009) *Dr B.R. Ambedkar: The Champion of Women's Rights,* Samyukta, A Journal of Women Studies.

Zelliot, Eleaner (1992). *From Untouchables to Dalit*, Manohar, Bombay.

5

Exploring Marginalised Men and Women in Hindi Cinema

Shamali Gupta Bose

Though the Varna (Caste system), dates back to the Aryan (Vedic) Age, following independence and the framing of our Constitution, it was hoped that the caste system would be invalidated by the Fundamental Rights which prohibited the discrimination based on Caste divide and propagated the right to equality. However, Caste continues to remain a prevailing force in the Indian society. Many may assert that the urban Indian society has overcome the ills of the caste conflict, the supposition is not totally correct. Even in urban privileged societies, caste plays a significant role. Inter caste marriages are prohibited to this day.

Popular cinema in India though, seldom focuses on social issues–leave alone the burning problem of casteism. If media is supposed to truthfully, impartially and dispassionately report and portray the documentation of conflict zones, then Hindi cinema, with its tremendous reach across the country, has sadly failed in its role of educating, informing and persuading society to bring about reforms. Most popular cinema highlights the urban upwardly mobile young, living in a rather escapist situation revolving around the protagonist and his arm candy heroine prancing around trees, sometimes surfacing from waves, singing inane songs accompanied by pelvic thrusting, semi clad dancers. On the other hand, the antagonist or most often, a group of bad men are out to ruin the world. The protagonist single handedly eliminates the bad men marries the heroine and lives happily ever after . . .

Unfortunately ground reality is far from the 'live happily ever after' syndrome. Honour killings happen even today to save the family from the so called disgrace of marrying outside the caste, and the same rage and revenge is depicted several times over in various Hindi commercial films. Yet there have been flashes of a few responsible Hindi films which have dealt with social issues, particularly caste conflicts or oppressions of the dalits.

One of the films I would like to contemplate on is the 1959 film directed by Bimal Roy '*Sujata*' based on a book by the same name written by Subodh Ghosh. This film explored the caste divide which is the poison of society as it catalyses discrimination, disparity and malignity. Made about 14 years post-independence, this film portrays the romance between an educated Brahmin man 'Adheer' and an untouchable woman 'Sujata'.

The film focuses on the oppression of the orphaned untouchable girl Sujata in a rigidly hierarchical, traditional society as it prevailed in India in those days. It provides a view of Sujata as a passive subject of gross discrimination: she is not allowed to study, she is kept away from social functions in her foster family's home as her very shadow is considered 'impure' by visiting relatives, tea prepared by her is shunned by almost all the family members except her broad-minded foster father, 'Upendranath Choudhury'.

In fact, one of the characters in the film, 'Pandit Bhawani Shankar Sharma', has this absurd logic to support his claim that Sujata be immediately thrown out of the house of Upendranath Choudhury. He says, "*Achyut ke tan se ek prakar ka gas nikalta hai jo kulin-o ke tan, man aur aatma ko dushit karta hai*". ('There is a strange gas emanating from the body of untouchables which makes the body, mind and soul of Kulins impure').

Fortunately, Upenbabu is fond of Sujata and cannot let her go into the bad world. Yet within the house itself there are ample instances that remind her that she is different. Even Charu,

Upenbabu's wife never ceases to hark back to Sujata that she is untouchable.

Adheer's love for Sujata however transcends the narrow restrictions of caste. He questions his grandmother, "Was Sujata not made by your God? No God or scripture has ever divided man on the basis of caste, religion or nationality..." He stresses Sujata had no control over the family she was born in...

The movie has director Bimal Roy using Gandhiji's fight against untouchability and the myth of Chandalika in Buddhism as its sub-texts to drive home his critique on untouchability in India as a blazing problem, leading to marginalisation of one segment of society. In fact, when traumatised by ostracism, Sujata contemplates suicide; it is Gandhiji's quote "*Mare kaise? Atmahatya karke? Kabhi nahiin? Aavashyakta ho to zinda rehne ke liye mare.*" that stopped her on her track.

In a master stroke, the writer has used the analogy of Gurudev Rabindranath Tagore's play *Chandalika* which is a visual presentation of the age-old struggle of the marginalised section of Indian society to accomplish the status of equality. It is based on a Buddhist legend associated with one of the Buddha's disciples named Ananda.

His magical words – 'Give me water' (*Jal dao aamaye, jal dao...*) – addressed to the frightened girl, Prakriti, significantly reverses her orthodox sense of being an outcaste and gives her a sense of freedom from bondage. By this 'water act', a new human being is born, who is full of vitality and energy and who revolts against this oppressive custom.

The educated young man narrates this story to awaken in Sujata a sense of purpose and realisation in equality of all human beings. Thus awakened, Sujata is emboldened to love Adheer and subsequently relinquish her love for the larger interest of her foster family.

A sudden accident, which leads to Charu's urgent need of blood of a rare group, shatters the entire myth of casteism. Nobody in the family shares the same blood group: only Sujata's matches.

By an irony of fate, the same Sujata who is considered untouchable, donates her blood, unconditionally, saves the life of her foster mother, leading to the final acceptance.

Benegal's first feature film, *Ankur* ('The Seedling', 1973), starring Shabana Azmi, Sadhu Meher and Anant Nag, explored economic and social disparities and sexual exploitation.

A few scenes for the film leave an enduring stamp in the collective memory of its viewers.

- The sense of harmony among the women belonging to a particular caste, when they all march together in a procession, to the temple of the divine Devi, in quest of a child. This opening scene where the women of the village offer seedlings to propitiate the Goddess sets the pace for the rest of the film.
- Rajamma tries to escape from an impotent husband who fails to give her the child she craves for. She is dragged back by her brothers-in-law and produced before the Panchayat. The decision of the Panchayat does not favour Rajamma. While the Panch passes its judgement, it says '*Aurat sirf Mard ki hi nahi, ghar ki bhi, khaandaan aur jaatwalon ki bhi hoti hai'*. In short implying that she is the property of all but herself and has no right to satisfy her own physical and mental longings. The husband is painted out to be a spineless person.
- A drunk Swami, keeps loosing in a game of cards until he pawns his wife, saying, '*Joru ko lagaunga–Mard ki aulaad hu…*' (I'll bet away my wife… after all I'm the progeny of a man"). The entire scene is reminiscent of the game of chaupar (dice) played between Yudhishtir and Shakuni, where Yudhishtir wagered his wife and changed the course of History.
- The main plot of '*Ankur*' of course revolves around Lakshmi and her husband Kishtaya who is a Kumbhar (potter belonging to a lower caste). Deaf and dumb, Kishtaya is also a chronic drunkard who is by a cruel turn of fate,

caught stealing toddy and publicly humiliated. Shamed, he leaves the village the same night. During Kishtaya's absence, Surya, the landlord's city-bred son who had earlier declared that he was above caste discrimination, takes advantage of Lakshmi's loneliness and gullibility by seducing her. A common refrain that he uses is '*main jaat-paat mein vishwas nahin karta*' (I don't believe in casteism). Yet when it comes to accepting Lakshmi's pregnancy for which he is responsible, he turns away fearing castigation from society. He is not man enough to accept responsibility for his own actions.

- On the contrary, the deaf and mute Kishtaya whom people had chastised, willingly accepts the innocent addition to the family and offers support to his wife.
- Benegal criticises the caste system and exposes the hypocrisies of the ruling class with no hint of didactical rhetoric or heavy-handedness. Symbolic of the struggle of the downtrodden individuals, there is nothing romantic about the sufferings of the worst atrocities that Lakshmi and her husband Kishtaya are subjected to.
- Hurt and battered, the couple return to their dilapidated dwelling, resigned to their fate. *Ankur* 'the seedling' firmly planted within her – the child she desired and finally gained. But 'the seedling' of popular upheaval sprouts at the end of the film in the form of the little boy who instigates a protest against the social hierarchy. The one stone this little boy throws is aimed at shattering the evils of a casteist society where its women are further marginalised and have to bear the brunt of all disgraceful actions.

We move to a more modern film with modern technology to support. Yet the nature of the struggle remains as it is in the case of caste, only the characters have undergone a change. The movie is '*Swades*', the village Charanpur and the protagonist Mohan Bhargava (Shahrukh Khan) the writer and director Ashutosh Gowarikar. Essentially the film revolves around NASA scientist–Mohan's quest to find his nanny, Kaveri amma. He finds her in village Charanpur and the problems faced by the villagers overwhelms him and he ends up looking for answers to their problems which are impediments to the growth and progress of the village. Besides, lack of water and electricity, illiteracy, and problems of casteism and prejudice against the lower strata of society are big barriers. He realises this when he finds that at a community screening of a film, the members of the lower caste are watching the film from the wrong side of the screen. There is a big divide which is amply demonstrated in the lyrics of the song, '*Yeh tara, who tara har tara.*

Dekho jisse bhi lage pyara, yeh sabh saath mein jo hai raat mein, to jagmagaya aasmaan saara

jo kisaan hul sambhale,
dharti sona hi ugaaye
jo gowaala gaiya paale
dhudh ki nadi bahaaye
jo lohaar loha dhaale
har auzaar dhul jaaye
mitti jo kumbhaar uthaale
mitti pyaala ban jaaye
sabh yeh roop hai mehnat ke
kuch karne ki chaahat ke
kissi ka kissi se koi bair nahin
sabh ke ek hi sapna hain
socho to sab apne hain
koi bhi kissi se yahan gair nahin
seedhi baat hai samjho yaara"

Ironically, those who do the most hard work are the most oppressed in society. The Kumbhars (potters) are the ones who tell Mohan Bhargava "*Hume sapney mat dikhaiye*..." (Don't make us dream...)

But he does make them dream, he makes the whole village dream–a magnificent dream of believing in themselves, of producing electricity, of going to school and of working together for the development of their own society. The narrative strongly brings out the fact that just as the members of the village united for the larger interest of bringing about a change in their lives, the nation too, which is at the crossroads could take a leaf out of their lives.

Development and empowerment are interrelated. Both are continuous too because development leads to empowerment. On the other hand education leads to the political, economic and social empowerment of women. In *Swades,* Gita is the epitome of women's empowerment. It's a blessing that her caste is not mentioned, because for an educationist, all narrow distinctions should not affect their vocation and commitment. Educated in Delhi, Gita is selfless in her effort to spread knowledge in the village. According to the Cambridge English Dictionary, 'empowerment' means 'to authorise'. In the context of human beings, they have to be authorised to have to be authorised to have control over their own lives, to speak up for their own rights. The character Birsa, an outcast, who lives on the outskirts of the village cannot dream of sending his children to school when he is not allowed to even enter the village. Kusum and Suman, the grand daughters of the village Panchayat are Class Four dropouts, not because of shortage of money but due to shortage of the will power on the part of family members. Haridas, the weaver, is unable to settle his debts and silently suffers inhuman discrimination. Against this backdrop, Gita stands out with her desire and dedication to ensure education for all. She even refuses alliance with a prospective groom whose family is against her working post marriage. She has the courage to say, "*ladkiyon ki hatheli sirf mehendi rachne ke liye nahi hoti*" (the palms of girls are not meant only for adornment with mehendi).

Gita's is that voice which speaks of a woman's *swabhimaan* (pride), *azadi* (independence) and *atmanirbharata* (self sufficiency) and stresses the need for spouses to share familial responsibilities. She also believes that education is the weapon that will bring about true emancipation of the downtrodden. She stands by Mohan in his endeavour to bring in uninterrupted electricity using indigenous methods and human resources from the village Charanpur. It is a victory of sorts for the village when the partially sightless old woman's bulb glows and her face glows too with delight when she says '*Bijli*' (electricity). 'Bijli' here almost becomes synonymous with progress through knowledge with the increased enrollment in school.

The journey into rural India is for the NASA returnee Mohan Bhargava, a metaphysical quest for HOME. 'Swades' hits home the fact that while we sit cocooned in the safe havens of our city dwellings, modern India is not very far from the 'reality' embodied by the village Charanpur, a HOME which is saddled with infrastructural impediments and social evils and gender biases. A fragmented social structure leads to alienation and marginalisation which hampers development.

Conclusion

While literature is a mirror of the society we live in, media, especially films can play an effective role to reflect the happenings in the society. Media has immense power in influencing and bringing about a radical social awareness and stressing the role of every individual in nation building. Instead of grabbing eyeballs the need of the hour is that media and particularly Indian cinema brings to the fore film makers and script writers who will weave in the harsh realities of society at the same time pressurise and criticise the drawbacks of the administration. Finally, a constructive parallel cinema can be instrumental in bringing about accord and harmony among the masses which includes men and women from all strata of society. As Swami Vivekananda had rightly said, "a nation which does not respect women will never become great…" Indian filmmakers need to remember this premise and portray women with the dignity they deserve.

Note

1. http://www.the-criterion.com The Criterion: An International Journal in English ISSN 0976-8165, Dr Prafull D. Kulkarni.

Videography

1. *Sujata*. Director: Bimal Roy (1959).
2. *Ankur* Director: Shyam Benegal (1973).
3. *Swades We the People* Director: Ashutosh Gowarikar (2010).

6

Dalit Woman and the Necessity of a Dalit Feminist Aesthetic Tradition

Runa Chakraborty

When has my life been truly mine,
In the home male arrogance
Sets my cheeks stinging,
While in the street caste arrogance
Splits the other cheek open.

(Rani WS, 22)

Perhaps nothing else could be more apt than these few lines to delineate the angst of a Dalit woman who is compelled to live a life of double sub-ordinations. Though Dalit movement has been successful in keeping the Dalit cause a burning issue, yet unfortunately, Dalit women remain invisible and their problems are relegated to the periphery in this wider struggle of the Dalit community to gain recognition. These women are Dalits among the Dalits since they are oppressed not only by the evils of caste discrimination but also by the politics of patriarchy. The fact of being born as women in low-caste communities makes them natural victims of sexism practiced by upper-caste as well as Dalit men. Owing to their low-caste status, these women are often considered by upper-caste men as 'cheap' or 'available' and hence are deemed 'fit' to be harassed, assaulted and raped.

Again, the threat of being physically or sexually abused by the men of their own communities makes Dalit women 'outsiders' within their own homes. The trauma and humiliation of sexual slavery along with the pain of back-breaking toil that Dalit women are often bound to endure are vividly documented by Bama- a Tamil Dalit woman writer as she narrates how her *periamma* was beaten to death by her husband since she was unable to satisfy his sexual hunger:

He wanted her every single day. How could she agree to his frenzy after she worked all hours of the day and night, inside the house and out? …when she refused, he practically broke her in half…. (Bama *Sangati* 10)

Marathi Dalit woman writer Baby Kamble's *The Prisons We Broke* (translated by Maya Pandit) also portrays a gruesome picture of domestic violence suffered by Dalit women within their own homes. Kamble writes:

Everyday the maharwada[2] would resound with the cries of hapless women in some house or the other. Husbands, flogging their wives as if they were beasts, would do so until the sticks broke with the effort. The heads of these women would break open, their backbones would be crushed, and some would collapse unconscious. But there was nobody to care for them. …Women led the most miserable existence. (Pandit 98)

Kamble's narrative informs us that the inhuman practice of chopping the nose of a 'wayward' daughter-in-law was rampant among the *Mahars*[3] till 1940s. These texts underscore the fact that the body of a Dalit woman is considered to be a convenient site for Brahmanism and patriarchy to exercise their power and authority. Owing to their caste and gender identities, Dalit women are often regarded as double non-entities. The contempt and indifference with which they are treated is made evident in *Sangati* as Bama describes the incident of a village meeting in which both women and men of her community took part. She writes:

"At once, a couple of young men got up and came towards us saying, 'Do you women have any sense at all? What are you muttering about here, when we men are talking seriously? Go home all of you". (Bama *Sangati, 21*).

However, we must remember that the purpose of Dalit women's literature is not to evoke pity from the readers. Neither Bama nor Baby Kamble drew a miserable picture of Dalit women in order to gain sympathetic support from upper-caste readers. On the contrary, Dalit women's writings are meant to assert their own identity and are pregnant with the potentiality of initiating a new genre of resistance literature within Indian literary milieu. It is relevant to mention here that Dalit writings-especially the life-narratives of Dalit male authors are largely silent about the trauma suffered by women within their own communities. For instance Omprakash Valmiki's *Joothan* which is otherwise a heart-rending account of humiliation suffered by low-caste people is marked by the absence of women. Again, those women who exhibit their agency in Surajpal Chauhan's *Tiraskrit* are portrayed in derogatory manner. (Beth). Moreover, Dalit women authors are often accused of weakening the integrity of Dalit struggle since they expose the sexism that exists within Dalit community. But we should remember that Dalit women have often been a prominent part of Dalit struggles since the time of Ambedkarite movement. Research conducted by Meenakshi Moon and Urmila Pawar revealed that Dalit women who participated in the Ambedkarite movement used to hold their own conferences and even passed resolutions against child marriage, enforced widowhood and dowry critiquing these practices as Brahmanical. These Dalit women showed remarkable strength and openness of mind while Dr Ambedkar called for the religious conversion. They supported it as they felt the need for a religion that would recognise their equal status. However, women's participation in the post-Ambedkarite phase of the movement marked a sharp decline except the major upsurge during the Land Right Struggle. Sharmila Rege questions this silence of Dalit women and asks "'Why is this different voice of the dalit women' inaudible in the two major new social movements of the 1970s, namely the dalit movement and the women's?" (Rege WS, 42).

The answer to this question may be found in the characteristics and the priorities of Dalit struggle that emerged in the 1970s. The vigor of Dalit movement which had lost its steam after the death of Dr Ambedkar, resurfaced again with the foundation of the Dalit Panthers in 1972. But in spite of its strong ideology and militant intentions, Dalit Panthers confined Dalit women "firmly in the roles of 'mother' and the 'victimised sexual being.'"(Rege WS 42). Similarly, women's movement of that period which made significant contributions to the analyses of work-related exploitation and violence against women remained absolutely silent regarding such issue as Brahmanism. The exclusion of Dalit women from the two major political and cultural movements of the 70s led to the complete erasure of their presence from the social discourse of the time. The fact that neither the Dalit struggle nor the 'mainstream' women's movement in India fore grounds the problems of multiple layers of oppression on Dalit women is evident in Urmila Pawar's autobiography: *The Weave of My Life*. Pawar writes:

"Women's issues did not have any place on the agenda of the dalit movement and the women's movement was indifferent to the issues in the dalit movement. Even today things have not changed. (Pawar, 260)"

The politics of categorising Dalits and women as two separate homogenous groups rendered Dalit women invisible and resulted in the propagation of such assumptions that all Dalits are male and all women are *savarna*[4] (Rege WS, 42). It is interesting to note here that a similar notion is also found in the discourse of black feminism where the process of homogenising such categories as race and gender relegate black women to the periphery.

However, the scenario in the Indian context changed during the 90s while several autonomous Dalit women's organisations upheld the issue of Dalit women's identity. The emergence of such organisations as National Federation of Dalit Women, All India Dalit Women's Forum, *Vikas Vanchit Dalit Mahila Parishad and Christi Mahila Sangharsh Sangathana* raised many political and theoretical questions besides criticising the Brahmanism of the women's movement and the patriarchal practices of Dalit politics. They ignited the fire of an ongoing debate which was set rolling by eminent critic Gopal Guru's essay, "Dalit Women Talk Differently" (1995). However, in Rege's opinion, Dalit women's movement should not be restricted to the act of naming the "difference" of Dalit women. It should, rather, develop a Dalit feminist standpoint. (Rege WS, 44). Standpoint theory prioritises the perspectives of the marginalised and hence a feminist standpoint epistemology proposes to make women's experiences instead of men's, the point of departure. Moreover, a feminist standpoint is essential to examine systematic oppressions in a society which according to standpoint feminists devalues women's knowledge. Hence, it can be inferred that implementation of Dalit feminist standpoint as an ideological tool will certainly be a revolutionary endeavor. The most liberating aspect of the standpoint of Dalit feminism is that it is not a static ideological position. Rege feels that this theory creates spaces for liberating interrogations because it is aware of the fact that "Dalit woman" is not a homogenous category and therefore is subject to constant interventions and revisions. Contrary to what Guru suggests, Rege proposes that non-Dalit women can 'reinvent themselves as Dalit feminists' though they cannot 'speak as' or 'for' Dalit women.

Here, it must be pointed out that the contemporary Dalit literature produced by Dalit women has performed a significant role in establishing this new standpoint. The unabashed frankness and the uncompromising tone of Dalit women authors underscore the fact that a new era of Dalit feminist consciousness has set in. However, in spite of such optimistic and favourable conditions, Dalit feminism has still not been able to form a distinct aesthetic tradition of its own. Sharan Kumar Limbale's book *Towards an Aesthetic of Dalit Literature* [*History, Controversies and Considerations*] explores the latent power of Dalit literature in subverting the hegemony of dominant systems of knowledge. It makes a comparative study between Dalit literature and Afro-American literature and opines that Dalit literature requires separate aesthetic principles to evaluate a Dalit writer. But Limbale's work does not focus on the need for a specific Dalit feminist aesthetic tradition that analyses Dalit women's experiences and addresses issues which exclusively touch Dalit women's lives. For example, can a Dalit woman's experience of sexual violence be adequately expressed through the general term 'oppression' which can be used as a parameter to understand and appreciate Dalit literature? What does a study of Dalit aesthetics reveal about the history of Dalit women writers? Perhaps answers to these questions can be found in the creation of a Dalit feminist critical tradition which can add meaning to Dalit women's movement in the same way as black feminist criticism has done to give African-American women an identity, a collective voice to protest and a distinct past to build their own future. In my opinion, there exists a close relation between the aesthetic traditions of these two marginalised communities and a thorough understanding of the black feminist criticism will help Dalit feminists create their own critical tradition.

Afro-American women, like their Dalit counterparts, suffer from continuing conflict of "loyalties and priorities" (Willis). They are forced to endure multiple layers of oppression as they are tortured not only by the racial-sexual violence of white men but also by the sexism of black men and the racism of white women. Neither the Black Liberation Movement nor the mainstream feminist movement bothered to talk about the predicament of black women because while the former emphasised on waging solely an anti-racist struggle, the latter concentrated on gender politics ignoring the problems involving race. The growing dissatisfaction with the practice of sidelining the issues of black women led to the emergence of black feminism in the US. The voice of protest against the politics of exclusion was heard in 1850s while the black woman activist Sojourner Truth in her landmark speech "Ain't I a Woman?" revealed how the concept of womanhood in America often accepted the white middle class woman as the standard. This tradition of protest that continued through eon has resulted in the flowering of a black feminist consciousness. Literary and critical writings of bell hooks, Audre Lorde, Toni Morrison, Maya Angelou, Alice Walker, Barbara Smith, Barbara Johnson, Patricia Hill Collins and many other writers and activists contributed to the development of this consciousness. Their purpose behind the formation of a black feminist criticism has been to create forms of knowledge based upon the experiences of ordinary black women since such theorisation would provide "unique angle of vision on self, community and society."(Bowles, Fabi, and Keizer). Black feminist critics have followed a two-pronged approach. On one hand, they engage themselves in an act of constructing a literary tradition by retrieving the lost writings of their predecessors while on the other; they carry on with their protest against the structures of violence that compel them to live in a state of subjugation. The seeds of black feminist criticism were sprouted during 1970s while two events—the women's movement and the black arts movement played a crucial role in preparing the ground for the emergence of black feminist consciousness. The growing visibility of Afro-American women and their significant impact on the contemporary black culture started being felt with the publication of August 1974 issue of *Black World* which coupled with the publication of Alice Walker's "In Search of Our Mother's Garden" in May 1974 marked a significant shift in the process of analysing women's creativity within the black American literary context. Mary Helen Washington in her essay "Black Women Image Makers" featured in the August 1974 issue of *Black world* professed 'we should be about the business of reading, absorbing and giving critical attention to those writers whose understanding of the black woman can take us *further'* (Bowles, Fabi, and Keizer, 7).

However, the meaning of black feminism surpassed Washington's emphasis on image making as Barbara Smith in her essay "*Toward a Black Feminist Criticism*" (1977) vehemently underscored the need for establishing a black feminist critical tradition since a feminist critical perspective can demonstrate the ways through which literature exposes the complex and brutal systems of oppression. Smith also stressed on the necessity of building a "body of black feminist political theory" (Bowles, Fabi, and Keizer, 9) since such a theory is essential in revealing the impact of the intersection of racism and sexism in black women's lives. A feminist political theory can also provide the white men as well as the black men and white women critics with a framework for analysing and responding to the works produced by black American women authors. The scenario improved by 1980s when a more mature consciousness invigorated the black feminist critical thought. It was manifest through the responses generated by Michele Wallace's *Black Macho and the Myth of the Superwoman (1979)* – a critique of sexism in the Civil Rights Movement and also through the reaction directed towards the sociologist Robert Staple's critical response to Ntozake Shange's play, *for colored girls who have considered suicide when the rainbow is enuf.* However, the confidence of being self-sufficient in asserting their identity oozed out as Audre Lorde said: 'black feminists speak as women and do not need others to speak for us'. (Lorde, 17). Deborah McDowell in her essay, "New Directions for Black Feminist Criticism" (1980) harped on the necessity of clear definitions and methodologies and also suggested that a critic should engage herself/himself in both textual and contextual analyses to interpret an Afro-American text since one should understand not only the linguistic nuances but also the text's historical and cultural background and the women's situation within it. Barbara Johnson's essay, "*Black Feminist Criticism*" (1983-84) focuses on a critic's function and comments that critics should expose their personal point of view instead of taking an objective stance. Limbale, too, in his essay on the aesthetic of Dalit literature pointed out the need for pursuing a contextualised study of Dalit literature with a subjective approach. Again, as in Dalit literary criticism, the question of the importance of the author's experience is also raised in the domain of black feminist criticism. While McDowell took up this issue and widened the sphere of critical discussions by asking whether black feminist criticism could be practised by black men, white women and white men, Michele Wallace in "*Who Owns Zora Neale Hurston*:

Critics Carve up the Legend"(1988) cautions against the possibility of misrepresentations which according to her rendered Hurston nothing but a commodity. All these debates, however, point towards the fact that black feminist criticism is a dynamic body of thought which keeps its horizon ever expanding through self-criticisms and constant reinventions. Johnson's statement 'what do we want to do anyway and for whom do we think we're doing it?'(Bowles, Fabi and Keizer, 19) explains why black feminist criticism has been successful in establishing itself as an important critical ideology within the domains of 'mainstream' literature and culture studies. The conviction of opening new avenues of discussions in the field of feminist-literary criticism becomes evident when Johnson proudly utters we might wonder…whether one might want to predict the day when other literatures will reflect the currents of the black American women's writing community." (Bowles, Fabi and Keizer, 19).

Dalit feminism requires such vigor and enthusiasm in order to develop a Dalit feminist tradition which will be the most effective means for Dalit women to assert their identities. The task of constructing a historiography of Dalit women writers will infuse the later generations of Dalit women activists and artists with a sense of firm rootedness in one's own tradition. Such a feeling, no doubt is extremely necessary for building the strong foundation of a promising future. Moreover, the parameters of Dalit feminist criticism will provide scholars and critics with tools to analyse the currents and the cross-currents of Dalit women's struggles. But it should also be remembered that these parameters are not supposed to be absolutely prescriptive because rigidity will certainly limit the flexibility of Dalit feminist literature which has the potentiality to be a part of the transnational feminist discourse that can turn their so-called 'local' issue into 'global agenda'. Like it's Afro-American counterpart, Dalit feminist literature should be incorporated within the gamut of 'mainstream' literature and should also force its way into the academia.

Dalit women's writings document the journey from subjugation to celebration. This will not be possible if Dalit literature as well as Dalit movement is not analysed, interpreted and evaluated by the theoretical assumptions of a Dalit feminist aesthetic tradition. Only then, it will be possible to translate into reality what Bama dreams in her life-narrative *Karukku* as she says:

"We must not accept the injustice of our enslavement by telling ourselves it is our fate, as if we have no true feelings; we must dare to stand up for change." (Bama *Karukku,* 25).

Glossary

1. Periamma-senior aunt.
2. Maharwada-The residential colony of Mahar community located outside the village.
3. Mahar-Name of an untouchable caste
4. Savarna-Term for a woman or a man of high caste.

References

Bama. *Karukku*. Trans. Lakshmi Holmstrom. Chennai: MacMillan India Ltd. 2000, Print.

Bama. *Sangati: Events*. Trans. Lakshmi Holmstrom. New Delhi: Oxford University Press, 2005, Print.

Beth,Sarah."Dalit Autobiographies in Hindi:the transformation of pain into resistance."1-11.Web.7.August.2011<http://www.sasnet.lu.se/EASASpapers/4SarahBeth.pdf.>

Bowles, Gloria, M. Giulia Fabi, and Arlene R. Keizer, eds. *New Black Feminist Criticism, 1985-2000 Barbara Christian*. Urbana and Chicago: University of Illinois Press, 2007, Print.

Challapalli, Swaroopa Rani. "Dalit Women's Writing in Telugu". Economic and Political Weekly (25 April 1998): WS 22, Print.

Collins, Patricia Hill. *Black Feminist Thought: Knowledge, Consciousness, and the Politics of Empowerment*. 2nd.ed. New York and London: Routledge, 2000, Print.

Guru, Gopal. "Dalit Women Talk Differently". *Economic and Political Weekly* (14-21 Oct 1995): 2548-49, Print.

Harding, Sandra. "Strong Objectivity: A Response to the New Objectivity Question". *Synthese* 104.3(1995): 331-49, Print.

Johnson, Barbara. "But What Do We Think We're Doing Anyway: The State of Black Feminist Criticism(s) or My Version of a Little Bit of History". *New Black Feminist Criticism, 1985-2000 Barbara Johnson*. Ed. Gloria Bowles, M. Giulia Fabi, and Arlene R. Keizer. Urbana and Chicago: University of Illinois Press, 2007, Print.

Kamble, Baby. *The Prisons We Broke*. Trans. Maya Pandit. Chennai: Orient Longman Pvt. Ltd, 2008, Print.

Limbale, Sharan Kumar. *Towards an Aesthetic of Dalit Literature [History, Controversies and Considerations]*. Trans. Alok Mukherjee. New Delhi: Orient Longman Pvt. Ltd., 2004, Print.

Lorde, Audre. "The Great American Disease". *Black Scholar* 10.8-9 (1979): 17, Print.

MacDowell, Deborah E. "New Directions for Black Feminist Criticism". *Black American Literature Forum* 14.4(1980): 153-59, Print.

Moon, Meenakshi and Urmila Pawar. "We Made History,Too: Women in the Early Untouchable Liberation Movement." *Gender and Caste*. Ed. Anupama Rao. New Delhi: Kali for Women, 2003, Print.

Pawar, Urmila. *The Weave of My Life: A Dalit Woman's Memoirs*. Trans. Maya Pandit. New York: Columbia University Press, 2009, Print.

Rege, Sharmila. "Dalit Women Talk Differently: A Critique of 'Difference' and Towards a Dalit Feminist Standpoint Position". *Economic and Political Weekly* 33.44 (1998): WS 39-WS 46, Print.

Shange, Ntozake. *For colored girls who have considered suicide, when the rainbow is enuf.* 1977. United States: Bantam Books, 1980, Print.

Smith, Barbara. "Toward a Black Feminist Criticism". *Conditions II* ii (1977): 25-44, Print.

Valmiki, Omprakash. Joothan: *A Dalit's Life.* Trans. Arun Prabha Mukherjee. Kolkata and New York: Samya and Columbia University Press, 2003, Print.

Wallace, Michele. *Black Macho and the Myth of the Superwoman.*1979. Verso: Verso Classics Edition, 1999, Print.

Wallace, Michele. "Who Owns Zora Neale Hurston: Critics Carve Up the Legend". *Village Voice* (April 1988), Print.

Willis, Ellen. "Sisters Under The Skin? Confronting Race and Sex". *Voice Literary Supplement* 8 (June 1982), Print.

7

Gujarati Dalit Writings: A Literature of Marginalised

M.B. Gaijan

Gujarati Dalits have sound and profound spiritual voice. But, due to untouchability, for centuries, that remained only heard in the untouchable's ghettoes, at the outskirts of villages. Still the tradition is maintained by the rural Dalits, still under the open sky at night, they sing the spiritual songs *Bhajans* with *Ektara*, the traditional typical musical instrument.

As literacy started and increased in the 20th century among the Gujarati Dalits, they started to write their saga sufferings and untold pain. Their secular voice becomes audible since before the independence. Dr Ambedkar and Gandhiji both remained the great force for Dalit/Harijan writings in Gujarat. In Gujarat Dr Ambedkar had served in Vadodara state for a short time that had remained great force for Gujarati Dalit writers to write from Ambedkarite perspectives. Under Dr Ambedkar's influence before the independence, Gujarati Dalits had started to cry against injustice and cruelty committed on them. Earlier it was in simple poetic form. Essays and stories were also composed in a simple language so the Dalit brothers could understand the message. But that remained marginalised.

But after Gandhiji's active efforts to emancipate untouchables from centuries old oppression and cruelty, the mainstream Gujarati writers highlighted the issue in their creativity. He renamed untouchables as *Harijan* and under *'Harijan Sevak Sangh'* he had started the mission to emancipate the unaccepted Hindu Humanity of the nation. Under Gandhiji's mega influence a novel literary trend started in Gujarat where *Harijan* was first time brought at the centre by the Non-Dalit Gujarati writers. The literature produced during 1935 to 1960 was mainly this sort of sympathisers writing which presented helpless, pitiable condition of untouchables so called "*Harijans*" the children of God.

But after independence as the literacy increased among Gujarati Dalits, the marginalised literary trend whose icon was Dr Ambedkar became alive again. Dr Ambedkar's philosophy, struggle, efforts were seriously studied and evaluated by the Dalits of Gujarat. As a result from the mid 70s the first generation of Gujarati Dalits has started writing, quite different from the mainstream Gujarati writings.

Gujarati Dalit writers' first prefer poem to express their emotions. The remarkable aspect of this writing is that it is created by Dalits and it is the furious cry against injustice, inhumanity and cruelty. Non-Dalits later on talk for Dalits in Dalits' tongue. At the earlier stage it was not noticed by the mainstream society.

Cruelty and killing of Dalits were/are not new things. There is law and orders but still injustice is committed on Dalits. At many places Dalits become victims of cruelty. Poet Chandu Maheriya in his poem writes 'How long they have to bear the chains of cruelty?

"How long you will bear these?
These cruel traditions of killing!
Started from the era of Rama Rajya,
That chain of brutality –
Does not stop now....
Even at the end of the 20th century......."[1]

Secular democratic Republic Indian is yet to be born where all are equal, no discrimination on the base of caste, class, race or gender. Still India is a community of castes, one is high, another is low, it is a society of caste-based capitalism, upper-caste-based capitalist class is at the top and lower-caste-based mass is at the last. In this condition powered-upper caste-based class obviously create injustice and cruelty on Dalits. It is a crude reality of Indian society. The orthodox class by using the fruits of science and technology in 21st century still they cherish centuries' old orthodoxy and hatred towards Dalits. So cruelty, injustice and boycott are going on. Gujarat is not the exception of that. Injustice and cruelty on Dalits are still going on.

Dalits should do cleaning job for the society (upper caste), this was the inhuman, spiteful religiously supported statement. Still the orthodox believe that Dalits must do their job – cleaning. But Kantilal Makwans' poem presents anger and protest;

> "In one direction I am standing and in another you are
>
> If I refuse cleaning what will happen to you?!
>
> Countless emerged the shit globules in the gutter
>
> which cannot be removed by spade,
>
> Their shapes are like *Tripunda*, *Trishulas*
>
> and some like lady's finger of month September,
>
> if I ask the charge at each globule it would be painful to you,
>
> If I refuse cleaning what will happen to you?!
>
> Since Valmiki who sink down while cleaning the gutter
>
> How can Moraribapu know the saga!!
>
> Who made us from poet to gutter cleaner?
>
> Find out those stories curved on the stone monuments,
>
> The crowds of cockroaches climb on the body
>
> And body shivers with the cold,

If I refuse cleaning what will happen to you?!"[2]

The poem is highly realistic. Gutter cleaning profession is mainly done by Dalits in Gujarat. There are many reasons behind accepting this cleaning work. Still a class of Dalits who does not have good education, no other work for their survival, they have to accept this filthy work. Gutter cleaning is a disgusting and dangerous work. While cleaning the gutters', many times cleaners die. When it comes in the news paper it becomes source for a Dalit poet. The poet has mentioned Moraribapu a leading Ramayana *Kathakar*. The poet writes in the poem the death of Dalits by suffocating while cleaning is not a new thing. It is started since long. For survival Dalits have to helplessly accept cleaning job but after understanding ideology they also started challenge and protest against unjust process.

Cruelty and injustice to women in general is still taking place in our society. Many times they are inhumanly treated. Their basic human rights are violated. They become victims of harassment, rapes and death. Dalit women suffer a lot, inhumanly, unbelievably. When she suffers nobody comes to help her except in some cases. Pravin Gadhavi's poem presents the pathetic truth in his poem "*Barter*";

"She was denuded and was paraded
In the public place of the village
Under the scorching mid day sun.
Neither she was a married woman nor a divorcee,
Neither she was a damsel nor a woman at her forty,
She was not a sex worker nor she was a woman
Her name was not in the electoral list.
She was not from any village,
She had no religion.
Nor she had tongue,
She had neither dignity nor honour,
Her sin was that by birth untouchable she was."[3]

The poet tries to picture the crude reality and helpless suffering of Dalit woman. These sorts of cruelty on Dalit women are reported many times. It is a fact of Indian society women suffer at two levels sometimes at home and many times at away from the home.

At the end of the poem, the poet is writing she suffers because of two factors, first she is a woman and second is she is a Dalit woman, so the poet writes "take back the constitutional Rights "Reservation" and give her human dignity, honour back to the Dalit woman."

Dalit woman is nothing but the untold saga of suffering, her one tragedy ends another begins. In this sort of life struggle they also try to cope with changing world of 21st century. They also express their feelings, thoughts through their creativity. Gujarati Dalit women writers' creation is note worthy. Daxa Damodara's poem *Anaconda* is highly realistic and novelty in literary world;

> "In the dark and deep jungle of anarchy
> Behind the dark and dirty mask of caste-ism
> On the branches of big and small trees
> With forked tongue
> Smells the blood of helpless being,
> Enormous and unable to move,
> Terrible and terrifying
> With a little chance rushes to attack
> Gallops..
> Moving twisting....
> Moving twisting....
> ....Helpless.
> Centuries after centuries have gone
> Why, still neither its hunger is satisfied nor it dies
> The Anaconda of untouchability?"[4]

The poem is a reality of our time. Caste plays very significant role in Indian society, at every stage of life, public and private, Gujarat is not an exception of that. Secular India is yet to be created. The poem suggests due to caste-ism untouchability becomes like a big boa-constrictor. Untouchablity takes different shapes in Indian society but totally it does not disappear.

Story is the second choice of Gujarati Dalit writers. Many Guajarati writers have written stories. A few of them are highly realistic and appealing. The stories written by Gujarati Dalits represent reality of rural as well as urban Gujarat. At both the places Dalits suffer differently because of being a Dalit.

Hasmukh Vaghela's story *Zol* (The Flame)[5] represents reality of rural Gujarat. In rural Gujarat still Dalit ghettoes are at the outskirt of the villages. Still the upper castes egoist orthodoxy is prevailing in the society. Dalits have to face the fact. Injustice and cruelty is taking place. The story opens with all members of the Dalit colony are extremely frightened because they are threatened by the *Darabara*, the upper castes to set fire on their houses. Kalubha, the son of *Sarapanch*, upper caste, he comes in the centre of Dalit colony and shouts demands Daliya, Daliya is a Dalit youth; "Son of pigs, if you love to live and love your wives-children, present Daliya here, otherwise whole colony will set on fire and will die alive" (Zol: 311). Understanding the terror of the event, the old Fuladosa begs to pardon Daliya for no reason. The old man told; "Bapu, Daliya is a child, pardon him....if you say, on behalf of him I take shoe in my mouth and beg you to forgive, *Bapa* please don't do anything wrong" (*Zol* :311-12). But Kalubha rudely abuses all.

The story presents picture of Holi festival of a village. At the evening on the Holi festival, at the outskirt of the village with the help of wood and cow/buffalo-dung cakes Holi was arranged. It was believed to set fire to Holi was/is the degraded work according to the mythical story of Prahalada and Holika. So in rural areas *Harijans* had/have to set fire to Holi. For that job they were/are given a little reward. In this story the Sarapanch orders Daliya to set fire to Holi, simultaneously he also orders to keep distance. Thus, untouchability is practiced. Daliya obeys the order and sets fire to the Holi.

The story further presents, on that evening *Darabars*, the upper castes come with iron-covered *lathis* and they form first circle around the Holi, then other castes and *Harijans* are at far away from the Holi. Coconuts are offered to the burning flames of Holi and who gets coconut from the flames of the Holi are known as the hero of the village. Kalubha, young man of the *Darabara* community is strong and sturdy, six feet in height. As a son of Sarapanch nobody dares to challenge him. He has also a strong body so he could get coconuts from the flames. So he is considered as a village-hero, a leader of his community.

In this story Daliya is a thin, weak Dalit youth. On that evening of Holi festival whoever gets coconuts is declared the hero of the village. Dalit cannot enter in this competition for village-hero. But here Daliya unexpectedly jumps and gets a baked coconut then runs away. That has raised fury among the *Darabara* community. They connect coconut catching issue with their honour. And to protect their honour they decided to destroy Dalits crops, set fire to Dalits' colony. It is the reason so Kalubha lost his temper and comes in the colony. He finds Kanku there. Kanku is Daliya's wife. She begs for Daliya's life. But blind by lust and fury Kalubha has denuded her, raped her. She cries for help but none helped her. She is left alone to cry and her house was set on fire. At late night Daliya returns to his colony. His house is burning and wife is crying. He could judge what has happened. Painfully helplessly he tells to Kanku; "Get up Kanku, we do not want to live on this land of cowards, stand up, let us go to the land where even coward air may not touch to our coming children". Telling this, holding hands of his wife the couple jumps in the fire of his house. To save their lives Dalits run away leaving their ghetto. The story is pathetic but based on reality.

Pathik Paramar's *Tejo Vadha*[6] is a very appealing story. The story presents crude, unbelievable reality. It is story of Tejo, a revolutionary Dalit youth who is appointed in as a teacher in very remote village of Gujarat. He is also a columnist. He has written two-three columns on the contemporary education condition and a few stories on political corruption. As a result of that he is posted in a remote village. While on other hand the political-flatters were appointed in schools nearby the city. In the village he is an unwanted teacher. Because of untouchabiliy discrimination is taking place. He thinks;

"Is it a village or cattle comp? Why a son of Harijan cannot teach the children of village? Only the upper caste can teach? Am I not a qualified teacher? If I teach them, will they be polluted? Why my drinking water pot is kept separated?"(*Tejo Vadha*: 15)

All these questions disturb him a lot. He feels continuously insulted. Villagers do not accept him as a teacher. He thinks;

> "I want to tell something but I can't. I cannot write. After throwing me in deep ditch of mud you become happy, aren't you? But I am like lotus flower in mud. My pan can't be controlled by any." (*Tejo Vadha*: 15)

The story presents predicament of Tejo. He thinks thus when he is walking at evening without anybody's company. In urban area it is tough for a Dalit to get a "good" house on rental base. In rural areas it is impossible. So Tejo gets a house in Dalit colony. At that particular evening, he gets very unpleasant experiences. There is ban on wine in Gujarat but reality is different. Takhubha, the upper caste, insults him and show a bag of wine. He walks on the rocky path where villagers rarely go.

When he reaches at the pit nearby the village where Dalit women are used to empty their bowls he sees Champa, his house owner's daughter. She is entrapped by Mangalsinh. Looking at Tejo, Mangalsinh becomes furious and rushes with knife at Tejo. He threatens to kill him.

Next day in the morning when he gets up late, he knew that a few Dalit women have secretly gone to fetch water from the well of upper castes. The upper castes *Darabars* knew the matter and they attacked on Dalit colony with weapons. As a result; "Three Harijans were killed on the spot, many injured. Deadly silence controlled the village." (*Tejo Vadha*: 17) The story presents there is no enough water facility for Dalits so the Dalit women secretly fetch water from the upper caste well. But the upper castes, as usual believe the well is polluted. Thus, cruelty committed on Dalits. Tejo thinks about the crude reality of the rural areas;

> "Theft, loots, killing, threatening, wine, quarrels, rapes, corruptions, caste-ism, sectarianism, classism, nepotism!....injustice and cruelty on Dalit women. Village is nothing but the place of sufferings. City is better than this." (*Tejo Vadha*: 17)

He also thinks that it is hell. He decides to leave the village but under the wrong FIR filed by the upper caste he is arrested by the police. The story presents crude reality. Still in rural areas untouchability based cruelty is taking place.

To portray the saga of suffering, the Dalit writers prefer novel form. A few Gujarati Dalit writers have given highly appealing, realistic novels. Joseph Macwan's *Stepchild* is one of them. It is translated into English. But still there are more Dalit novels written in English. Harish Mangalam's *Aganzal*[6] (The Flames of Fire) is an autobiographical novel. It is a story of protagonist, Veeru. His family members, Dalits' condition in villages everything is minutely and realistically presented. The novel presents practice of untouchability in rural areas. The novel presents the picture post independent era but still untouchability is existing in many forms. When Veeru was in standard Seven at that time, about the school novelist writes;

> "So called upper castes teachers were not teaching to Dalits' children. The ghost of untouchability was dancing everywhere. ….Farmers were thinking; 'after getting education if Dalits will get job then who will do labour in our farms"……… Dalits'

> condition was worse than animals . . .. Upper castes were calling them by names. They were standing even away from the shadows of Dalits. Because of the fear of being polluted the upper caste teachers were throwing sticks at them." (*Aganzal* :16)

In this sort of adverse condition Veeru struggles. Right from the childhood he prefers rational and revolutionary path. He establishes a library and finds only learning is the best means for Dalits' emancipation. The novel presents the journey, how a rural Dalit youth emerges from nothing to something.

Daxa Damodara is a mature young Dalit woman writer. Her novel *Savitri*[7] is an excellent work of art. The novel presents life story of Jotiba Phuley and Savitribai Phuley. The writer has re-interpreted Indian history and re-created the struggle of Savitribai and Jotiba. First girls' school for untouchable was started by this couple. They had established "*The Satya Shodhak Samaj*", *Bala Hatya Pratibandhaka Gruha* (A Home for the pregnant mothers, they were allowed give birth of babies, if they wished they could get their babies or leave it in the home) and library. It is story of Savitribai. She struggles right from her childhood. As a faithful and committed companion she always remains with Jotiba in his life mission. After his death she tries to fulfill his uncompleted dream. While serving the plague victims, especially Dalits, she becomes a victim of bubonic plague and dies. The novel has sound bases so it can be evaluated from different angles.

Recently published novel *Vajra Prahar*[8] by Kantilal Parmar presents reality rural life. Practice of untouchability and cruelty on Dalits are presented in the novel. Because of cruelty Dalits migration is also highlighted in this novel.

After evaluating Gujarati Dalit writings, a few remarkable aspects clearly emerge before the readers:

- There is anger, protest, and struggle for identity – in their creativity they justify why there is anger, protest, and struggle.

- Cultural assertion.
- Demand for justice, equality, human acceptance.
- Contribute in nation building-environment, education, corruption, social service etc.
- Contemporary cruel realities, injustice, boycott, killing of Dalits are highlighted in their works.
- Dalit have their own media to present their voice. Still accepted by the mainstream. Thus it is the voice of marginalised even in the early 21st century.

References

1. Maheriya Chandu, *Asmita*: Khet Vikas Parishad, Khet Bhavan, Ahmedabad, 1984. p. 51.
2. Makwana Kantilal, *Nai Upadu Mathe Melu* (*I'll not Carry Dirt on My Head*), Hayati, ISSN 2231-0282, Gujarat Dalit Sahitya Akademi, Dec. 2012, p. 5.
3. Gadhavi Pravin, *Barter*, in *Dalit Vani*, ed. by Harish Mangalam, Gujarat Dalit Sahitya Akademi, Ahmedabad, 2006, p. 23.
4. Damodara Daxa, *Anaconda*, in *Bharatiya Dalit Naree Lekhan* ed. by Faruk Shah, Hayati, ISSN 2231-0282, Gujarat Dalit Sahitya Akademi, March. 2012, p. 43.
5. Vaghela Hasmukh, *Zol* (The Flame), in *Varta Lok*, ed. by Harish Mangalam, Pathik Parmar, Madhukant Kalpit, Arvind Vegada, Gujarat Dalit Sahitya Akademi, Ahmedabad, 2008, pp. 311-318.
6. Mangalam Harish, *Aganzal* (The Flames of Fire), Gujarat Dalit Sahitya Akademi, Ahmedabad, 2007. p. 16.
7. Damodara Daxa, *Savitri*, Gujarat Dalit Sahitya Akademi, Ahmedabad, 2008.
8. Parmar Kantilal, Vajra Prahar, Gujarat Dalit Sahitya Akademi, Ahmedabad, 2012.

8

Plural Resistances in Dalit Autobiographies

Kanchan Verma

But in Order to make
You understand, to give
You my life, I must
Tell you a story

Virginia Woolf, The Waves

The lives of autobiographers are elaborate in nature. This comes in with its own perils. They open their hearts and speak their minds in order to be understood by the readers. However, in return readers counter the self-assertion of the writer with their own. An autobiography is a kind of writing which, compared to any other genre, tries to narrow down the distance between the writer and the reader. It is a text that seeks to draw us into itself without any kind of reservation and seems to address us with intimacy and honesty. For a common reader, it is a unique self-presentation of an author, some famous public figure who is known to him and about whom he wants to know more. The common reader does not normally read the autobiographies of authors who are unknown to him. An autobiography is a certificate of a unique human passage through time. It is a text inhabited by a living person, an author, who was present to himself while he was writing becomes present in front of us as we read. It is a record of the past in its most transparent form.

'Autobiography represents an effort made by those who write it at the integration of their past lives and present selves: The autobiographer wishes to stand forth in print in the form of a whole.'[1]

The author tries to create a face in words by which he can be recognised by others, different from the rest. In other words it is a pictorial representation of himself.

'Autobiography does not indeed aspire to delineate the features of his personal history and character which the author believes are his claim to distinction, so that his text can finally take place of his person, as a tangible evidence of his identity.'[2]

An autobiography is a medium that represents and reports the inner life as well as the life outside by which the former has been conditioned. One can say this with conviction that in most instances, it is the exchange between his own self and the society in which he lives, that becomes the guiding theme. For him and for us there is something waiting to be revealed in the fullness of time.

Per Strounbjerg rightly believes that the genre (autobiographies), does not prescribe what it should be but rather emphasises on what it should be read as. This brings us to the number of common traits in autobiographies. According to Philippe Lejeune –

'It's a narrative prose where the perspective of the narrator is retrospective. The protagonist is identical with the narrator and the identities of the protagonist and the narrator must be that of the author. Most important of all the subject treated in an autobiography is the life of the individual, with the accent put on the development and history of the personality.'[3]

Historically, the portrayal of Dalits in literature, since time immemorial, has been full of distortion and contradictions. Realistic and accurate portrayal has been lost in the writings of the elite which is highly imaginative in nature and far from authentic. Dalits are often shown as vile-natured, filthy, mongolite clowns whose only use in the society is for menial purposes. The picture is often repulsive, distorted, inaccurate and highly maligned. Therefore, Dalit writers have taken up the responsibility to put their pains and problems in words and express their feelings through their writings, so that the world understands the shameful and inhuman life that is imposed on Dalits. What better way can one find than the autobiography which is highly appropriate for relating experiences.

It is the most successful and intellectually stimulating form which is both eloquent and reflective. It has the liveliness of a tale as well as the power to amuse and provoke. Unfortunately, it has always been in the domain of the elite class.

'*Apne-Apne Pinjare*' (1995), is the first autobiography in Hindi to have been written by a Dalit. Autobiographical reflections were found in several earlier works, as well, but they all came from the elite classes so they were distant and removed from the concerns and experiences of the people at the bottom of the caste pyramid. When the idea of writing an autobiography came to their mind, the moment itself is in the form of resistance. It is also a way of showing resistance against the elite because the genre of poetry or story was prevalent across various divides of the caste system where as writing an autobiography was something which was untouched and untried. It has a sense of achievement, accomplishment and giving back to the society in itself. It has a sense of pride as the only people who are well established in the society have been writing their autobiographies. Now this can also be seen as a form of resistance, which comes from the sentiment 'I can also write' or 'A Dalit can also write' his autobiography. The question that arises in their mind is why does only a Tagore, Nehru, Gandhi or a person from the elite class have the avenue to write about their lives? Why not a Dalit?

It is easy to express oneself in an autobiographical form because of its expressiveness. It is the experience of 'I', instead of the writer writing in the third person where, it is difficult to find one's own voice in an autobiography. There is a direct relationship between the writer and his experiences that are being narrated. It is about his own society, joys and sorrows, pains and sufferings. It is a documentation about his life and times which is pure action, not imagination. In other literary genres authenticity is the problem. Most of the time the imagination is elite or the sources on which their work is based are inherently unreliable. There can never be an 'ultimate' truth of 'private fact' or feeling. Most of the material is reinvented whereas an autobiography is the mirror of life based on the personal and intimate feelings of an author, an ideal of human, moral truth.

Omprakash Balmiki, a Dalit Writer in the preface of his autobiography *Joothan*, Writer:

> 'The pains of Dalit life are intolerable and difficult to experience. These experiences have got no place in literary expression. We have breathed in such social order that is very cruel and inhuman and is also insensitive towards the Dalits.'[4]

The author tried many a time to pen down his experiences but could not succeed. After writing an editorial note for an edited book, he finally decided to write. He found:

> 'There were several dangers in writing these experiences. I started writing in a systematic way after a long period of struggle within. This led me to relive atrocities, exploitation and deprivation. In this process, I experienced tremendous mental torture. I felt how painful it is to unlayer myself. Some people consider it unbelievable and exaggerated...but why should there be any doubt to pen down what is truth?'[5]

> Another Dalit writer, Sheoraj Singh's '*Bechain*', expressed his experience while writing his autobiography, *Mera Bachpan Mere Kandhon Par*, as, 'a seal of life just like the touch of an untouchable ...even more than this.'[6]

Autobiography is documentation of life and its struggle. One can see it comprehensively covered by the author, Mohandas Naimishrai. The dedication of the book gives an insight 'a black and white document of struggle of my life, dedicated to all those who got associated and disassociated with me having feelings of happiness and sorrow.'[7] Therefore an autobiography becomes the narration of the hardships and undignified life of Dalits who are in search of their identity. It is also a narration of their resistance to the oppressive society which is unjust and discriminatory.

In elite writings, Dalits are portrayed as meek, mute and pathetic objects or tragic figures, unable to resist any oppression, and therefore born sufferers. *The God of Small Things* by Arundhati Roy or *A Fine Balance* by Rohinton Mistry are classic examples in this category. It is written in an appropriative voice, a voice that contains, but does not expresses Dalit experience. Dalit autobiographers speak about the realities and contradictions of the elite society where people live in almost a permanent mode of denial.

It is a way of challenging the hegemony of high caste so that 'other voices' may also be heard, thus creating a space for themselves.Though, autobiography is the favourite genre of Dalit Writers, it is facing severe criticism from the mainstream critics on issues such as-

- Autobiography as not a literary genre.
- Literary characteristics of the narratives.
- Unstructured, artless outpourings of writers unmediated experience.
- Repetitive and stereotypical.

In defence, Balmiki quotes Das, 'Dalit writers should write autobiographies so that not only our history will stay alive, but also our true portrayals of wrong doers. Dalit autobiographies will provide inspiration to our future generations'.[8] According to another Dalit writer Kancha Ilaiah, autobiographies are '...indeed the

most authentic way in which the deconstruction and reconstruction of History can take place.'[9] To sum up, Arun Prabha Mukherjee rightly opines that it is not just remembering the past but shaping it in a way which would in turn help to understand the life of the person and the social order that shaped it, bringing wider understanding in the minds of readers. It is not mere reportage but the 'authencity of experience as being the most important characteristic.'[10] By writing their autobiographies, Dalits have established themselves as a subject in literature which was not happening before. Therefore, in a way, they have 'broken new ground, mapped a new territory.'[11]

Post modern critics propose that, truth in Dalit autobiographies is often 'constructed' and the narrator presents himself in a way he feels comfortable by 'reprocessing' his memories. But Dalit autobiographies pose challenges to them because these autobiographers have named people and places in the text by their real names. Therefore, it is a testimony and should be given the status of documented Dalit History. One can see it in Mohandas Naimishrai 'Apne-Apne Pinjare' Balmiki's '*Joothan*', Bechain's '*Mera Bachpan Mere Kandhon Par*' or Tulsiram's '*Murdahiya*'.

Autobiographies have always been written by the mighty, rich, famous and the glamorous. It is out of the ambit of the ordinary, average, the commoner. One of the most successful and intellectually stimulating genre which is both expressive and reflective, it has the liveliness of a tale as well as the power to amuse and provoke. Unfortunately it has always been in the domain of the elite class. So, when a Dalit, a person on the margin plans to write his autobiography, isn't this also a form of resistance?

Dalit autobiography is the story of the life that is vulnerable and powerless, full of struggles and hardships. It is a must read for those who are concerned about the people on the margins and the voiceless. Prominent in their writing is the idea of rejection of established norms, revolt against elite notions. One may call it a literature of resistance, rejection and rebellion. But why is this resistance? Against whom is this resistance? How do 'they' resist the elite? What kind of resistance does one come across while reading these autobiographies? What do they gain and what is lost in the entire process of resistance? How does the new generation of young, highly educated Dalit youth resist/rebel compared to the old guards of their society? Does it only entertain us or also provoke us? Does it only talk or also make us reflect on to the society of it's time?

In my paper, I would try to look into the possible answers of these questions in the politico-socio-economic context. With this important question that needs to be answered is the language of resistance i.e. how language has been used as a tool to resist/rebel by the dalits, against the elite and their system? My paper would therefore be an examination of the appropriation of the form of autobiography and the variety of resistance that come with this form of writing.

For my study, I have taken four autobiographies written in Hindi. They are-

(i) *Apne-Apne Pinjare* by Mohandas Naimishrai, Vani Prakashan, New Delhi, 1995.

(ii) *Joothan* by Omprakash Balmiki, published by Radhakrishana Pvt. Ltd., New Delhi, 1997.

(iii) *Mera Bachpan Mere Kandhon Par* by Prof. Sheoraj Singh '*Bechain*', published by Vani Prakashan, New Delhi, 2009.

(iv) *Murdahiya* by Dr Tulsi Ram, Published by Raj Kamal Prakashan, New Delhi, 2012.

Looking at the wide canvas of autobiography, there are certain things which are common in all four of them. I would like to highlight them and then take up the main issue of resistance separately.

- The autobiographies provide us with rare and indeed rich glimpses of everyday activities of the people who are living on the margins of the society.

- They also provide us with the social and the cultural milieu within which these activities shaped their experiences and consciousness, their emotions and identities, their day to day chores and hardships of their life.
- The range of themes that the author covers in their autobiographies are vast. From their childhood ventures, youth and adolescent, wonderings, frailities and weaknesses, hardships struggle, relationships to the significance of women in their lives.
- They are forthright about their views on religion and social norms and open about their doubts and sceptcism.
- Dalit autobiography is the story of a life that is vulnerable and powerless, yet full of struggles and hardships. It is a must read for the people who are highly concerned about the people on the margins and the voiceless.
- The humble background of the authors provide them the courage to admit to their frailities and shortcomings. It is a honest and reliable account of their lives because they have not tried to hide those things where there behaviour was less than exemplary.
- Authors have portrayed the sorrows, tribulations, poverty and ridicule endured by Dalits. Irrespective of everything done by them they aim to work tirelessly to make the society a better place for everyone leading towards total revolution.
- Prominent in their writing is the idea of rejection of established norms and the strong impulse of revolt against the elite notions. One can see resistance in their writings.

The Sufferer and the Perpetrator – Cause and Consequence of Dalit Resistance: Background

There was a fundamental change in the lives of the people as a result of India's Independence. It brought hope to the lives of the millions with its public welfare schemes and five-year plans. But, soon all hopes of the people were thwarted because of growing poverty, unemployment, religious frenzies, communal conflicts and corruption in each and every sphere of public life.

In North India, the process of bringing Dalits actively under one umbrella started in 1980s, although it was in it's initial phase in the mid-1960s. There were many factors such as the defeat and decline of Congress after the 1967 elections and the entry of backward classes in the political arena. With the formation of "Bahujan Samaj Party" in 1984, one can see a marked difference in the increased political mobilisation and consciousness of the Dalit Community. It provided a common platform to all deprived sections of the society.

One can see the change from resistance to Dalit assertion as a result of continuous mobilisation and participation, which enhanced the political consciousness and participation among the Dalits. The question of Dalit identity was born from the womb of Dalit consciousness, clearly mentioned by Sudha Pai:

> 'Dalit identity has two faces, neither of which can be described revolutionary. One under the leadership of the BSP believes that capturing state power and introducing policies favourable to Dalits from above can best serve Dalit upliftment. It is elitist, conservative and election oriented and aims at political empowerment of Dalits. The other represented by the micro-level process of Ambedkarisation functions within civil society to protect the interest of Dalits through collective social organisations. It believes that spreading the message of Ambedkar through various methods of grassroots mobilisation such as education and building awareness will in time introduce social transformation.'[12]

This led to the emergence of Dalit literature in the Hindi belt in 1980s. With its raw energy and earthy flavour, Dalit writers presented in their writings, the conditions and the issues of poverty the caste system and struggle against conditions of existence. While injustices, atrocities and physical repression intensified, the educated Dalit writers gave vent to their feelings in the protest literature and it acted as a 'catalyst' to the on-going Dalit assertion, movement for mobilisation, identity and empowerment.

Dalits have voiced their dissatisfaction against discriminatory Hindu caste system. They derive their strength from the thoughts of Baba Saheb Ambedkar and rebel against such a system which does not recognise the value of a human being as its seminal value. Personal experiences are the basis of such writings, where there is revolt against such notions and rejection of the values that strip a human being of his dignity. Dalits write with a purpose and that is

> '...Society may change and understands its problems. Their writing articulates this impatience with intensity'.[13]

One can see a similarity in the writings of Dalit writers because their experiences are similar. The experiences of an individual appears to be that of the community. Every member has undergone the inhuman torture numerous times in his life as the tortures of the society against Dalits have been the same.

> 'Social boycott; separate *bastis*; wells and cremation grounds; inability to find rental accommodation; The necessity to conceal caste; denial of admission to public places; injustices done to Dalit women; dragging and cutting of dead animals; and the barber refusing to cut hair – These experiences are alike for all Dalits'.[14]

Traditionally Dalits dealt directly with member of higher castes. However they were expressed to observe various proprieties in their presence. With the passage of time, this is changing considerably, especially among younger men and women, depending on the degree of economic dependency and political consciousness.

The youngsters are politically conscious and do not show any meek worship to the elites. Times have changed and they are not as ignorant as the olden days. The political parties have taught them about their rights and the young generation of Dalits have started developing a contempt for the higher castes. This represents a challenge to the caste system and also an increased awareness of one's own group as a political entity.

Unfortunately, religion which ought to elevate man to a higher spiritual plane has constantly ended up in debasing him. Idol worship, animal and human sacrifice, religious bigotry, fanaticism, barbaric primitive practices, priesthood, untouchability, etc., were the evils strongly rooted in Hindu way of life and therefore morbid for all practical purposes. The orthodox religion hindered the growth of man and was devoid of humanistic values like charity, morality, pity, benevolence, virtue and strengthening of bonds of love and harmony between men of different religions, caste and creed.

The autobiographies show that the writers mind was working powerfully on the subject of baseless rituals or sacrifices which were a popular component of Hinduism. The writers strike with all their might at the root of evil rites and follow the religion of love, compassion and universal brotherhood.

Dalits are not allowed to participate in Hindu religious celebrations. Not only this, they are also discriminated in the temples because they are deemed as untouchables whose touch will contaminate the elites. Humiliated and look down upon by the elites, Dalits revolt against the Hindu religion and boycott religious texts, scriptures and symbols.

As rightly described by Dr Ambedkar caste system is a multi-storey building without doors and ladders with it's inmates in every storey bound to die in the same storey. It is practically dead for every reason, Dalits have to pull it down by force.

Irrespective of its simplicity and complexity every culture has its own beliefs and practices concerning religion. The supernatural powers are identified with a group of powerful forces and deities which control and influences the happenings in the community. Thus, Dalits have specific Gods for health, disease, calamity, prosperity and so on. All these deities have their own respective areas of influence, effect and control as well as nature of action. Depending on the cause of the illness, services of the Ojha/ Bhagats are sought after in worshiping the deities and when epidemics or disease erupt in the village, he offers a sacrifice at the sacred place. He is entrusted with the benevolent deities and the spirits are controlled by him often through magical performances. The ailing person is often beaten by chains, sticks or brooms to cure him. There is a strong belief in them that they would be cured by the invisible powers. Although, the existence of the Primary Health Centres in the neighbouring areas of the villages has considerably changed the attitude of the villagers towards disease and their treatment but people still believe that the diseases are the result of the wrath of some spirits. So, to propitiate the spirit, some sort of magical practices are observed. It may be relevantly noted that the educated Dalits have given up almost all their traditional beliefs and practices that follow the principle of any kind of physical or mental harm to themselves or to any other individual.

Dalits reject Hindu methodology as *Manuwadi* and anti-Dalit as stated by Dangle, 'The tradition and culture of ancient India does not contain anything which a Dalit can own with Pride.[15] Kancha Ilaiah retells the stories from the sacred Hindu mythological text from Dalit point of view. He says, 'Hinduism differ from other religions even in terms of the way it has structured it's Gods and Godessess. All the Gods and Goddesses are institutionalised, modified and contextualised in a most brazen anti-Dalit Bahujan mode'.[16] Therefore, Ancient Indian Texts have been irrelevant for Dalits.

The God and the Goddesses of Dalits are different in a sense, they are not killers and oppressors of weak and subdued. They can be approached by anybody, without the meditation of a priest, in their own language rather than Sanskrit, unlike Hindus. There are no distinction of caste or class in any form as far as worship is concerned. War and violence is not the central philosophical notions of Dalit people unlike Hindu Gods who are basically war heros, whose ultimate aim is to create a caste based society, based on exploitation and inequality. The sacred texts of Hindus are based on unjust and inhuman treatment of Dalits. Thus, Ambedkar had burnt *Manusmriti* which was a powerful symbolic act of resistance. Dalits don't respect the Vedas and other sacred texts of Hindus.

Caste has functioned and continues to function as a very effective system of economic exploitation. This caste system has also prevented the formation of social classes with common interest or purpose.

Economic conditions of Dalit families are pathetic. Majority of them work in the lands of the 'Savarnas' as bonded labour/ paid labour in the cultivable land. But, at the same time they have to supplement their family income by doing other work which is essentially menial in nature. They also work, either as permanent or as casual labourers, which is never sufficient to fulfill the basic needs of their everyday life. They are not only heavily indebted in debt but even for getting loans, are dependent on the high caste people to act as guarantors. It is a vicious cycle in which they were trapped because even after paying back the principal amount with interest, are victimised by the cunning manipulation of the *Banias* who make their life pathetic. 'Begar' was another problem, which if not performed brought unimaginable suffering and misery to them. It was an established norm in the village and people never questioned it because elites often argued that Dalits have always accepted their position and surrendered themselves to the mighty. But, it is quite clear that it was the superior economic and political power of the elite that kept the lower ones suppressed.

Village mohallas were settled along the caste-lines. One can see higher caste people residing at the heart of the village which is also the focal point of all important activities, followed by middle caste houses. The southern part of any village mohalla was assigned to the people doing 'contaminous' work, with separate cremation grounds and wells. There was much dissimilarity between the high caste living in the village and the untouchables living outside the boundary of the village.

The genesis of Dalit literature can be traced way back in the 'timeless literature' of the medieval Saints. For them attaining 'Moksha' was more important then the compelling social problems of those on the margins. The birth of a person in a particular caste was the result of their previous 'Karma'. They did not struggle against the caste system as such. However, Saints sympathised with the *Shudras*. There was a sense of helplessness in them. It was desire for mercy, expressing pain and arousing feeling of pity. This is marked as the first phase. Today, the Dalits have broken way from Hindu culture and kept themselves aloof from the Saints. One can see the cultural shift that has taken place since the time of the Saints.

Dalits reject the established culture and traditions of the elites and claim the tradition of Buddha, Kabir, Phule and Ambedkar. Cultures and tradition develop with the passage of time with the exchange of ideas-new and old and out of the 'negation of the old' acquire their independent existence. Today, Dalits do not want sympathy and compassion, but want to live with self-respect, dignity and honour with their cultural identity intact. Burning of '*Manusmriti*' and other epics were ways of showing their dissatisfaction against the elite writings which did not accept them as one. Dalits reject the traditions and religions that do not regard the self-respect of a person that leads to a rebellion against overbearing religions and traditions. There is an open revolt against the hypocrisy of the elite in the garb of sympathy attitude towards Dalits.

Cultural context is depicted through community festivals, rituals and community get togethers. There is a reference to the 'Ambedkar Jayanti' and 'Ravidas Jayanti' celebration and its festive preparation by the Dalits, which was a big occasion to celebrate. Ideally everyone should be a part of such celebrations irrespective of caste or class. But the author noticed a very strange thing – absence from such celebrations by the elite members on one pretext or another. This kind of behaviour of Savarnas made the author think about his own identity vis-a-vis others in the caste based Hindu society. He writes-

> 'I tried hard to talk to them about the anomalies but they didn't show any interest. They would talk behind my back and used bad words about Ambedkar. Hearing all this, I would lose my temper. In the end, I started boycotting their religious functions.'[17]

Here, we see that the author tried to talk to the elite but when given cold shoulder then he had no alternative but to resist to their sick mentality by boycotting their functions, which were of prime importance to them. The author started participating actively for Dalit cause and formed a separate theatre group performing plays and organising exhibitions, which were progressive in nature and showcased the works of Dalits. In this way, he showed his resistance to the oppressions of the educated and culturally dominating elites and provided an alternative to Dalit performers by forming his own group of performing and literary art.

Dalit literature is a literature of resistance, rejection and rebellion. The resistance is against those beliefs and traditions which are illogical and irrational for the society in general and mankind in particular. Both the oppressor and the oppressed lived in the same village/city, breathed the same air, yet the behaviour of the mighty and powerful Elite has been shameful. The way they treated Dalits, would be unbelievable by today's yardsticks. Dalits were deprived of basic human rights time and again. The only thing they could do was to resist the tortures meted out to them by the mighty Savarnas, at times openly and mostly quietly. The resistance was a way of their struggle for survival. With the passage of time they formed groups, gathered together, consolidated their power, openly revolted against the system which is dead for all practical reasons.

'Joothan', Apne-Apne Pinjare, Murdahiya and *Mera Bachpan Mere Kandhon Par* are the classic examples of Dalit resistance literature in which we can find various incidents of oppression by the mighty and its counter resistance by the Dalits. One can find anguish and anger in these writings against the established norms of the society.

Omprakash Balmiki describes his childhood in a small village in Muzaffarnagar in Uttar Pradesh, 'in an atmosphere characterised by stuffed narrow streets, pigs, half-naked children, dogs, daily quarrels and acute poverty.'[18] This stands true for every Dalit autobiographer. Their journey was filled with strife and discrimination. The working class, who work for others, is forced to live in such inhumane conditions.

After great difficulty he get admitted at the local village school where he is exploited by his teachers and peers who make fun of him. He is forced to sweep the floor everyday instead of getting a chance to attend his classes. He does not lose heart but continues with the work. This was a tactic of elite teachers so that he would eventually run away from the school. In this Episode, Balmiki doesn't forget to mention the resistance shown by his father to school authorities against the exploitation his son underwent.

> 'My father took the broom from my hand and threw it away. His eyes were red with anger...He started yelling, "Where is that teacher, the son of Dronacharya, who makes my son sweep the floor..." His voice echoed in the school, hearing which Headmaster and other masters came out. Kaliram master abused my father and threatened him but my father was not bothered. I could never forget the way my father spoke to the Headmaster with Courage... Headmaster shouted at the top of his voice, 'get lost with him... A chuhda wants to study... get out... or I will break your hands and limbs.
>
> My father held my hands and moved towards home and made himself heard to the Headmaster, 'you are a teacher that's why I am going...just remember this... This son of a Chuhda will study in this school itself.. and not only he, but others like him will also come in the future'.[19]

Dalits resist against any kind of oppression and oppose injustice done to them either on a personal level or to their community at large. The old guards fully know that the future of their children is safe, when they get education. Even the repetitive abuse by the elite, could not deter the author's father from raising his voice. He fully knew that only educated people can help in uplifting the society. Thus, he always encouraged the author to study.

The author's father also retaliated against the practice of 'Salaam' and stopped it—a custom in which newly wed couples from Dalit castes went to the homes of these whose families they were employed to pay respect and in return got some money, clothes or food. It was a ploy of upper caste people to humiliate and lower their self esteem forever—a way to create an inferiority complex in the minds of young ones, to crush the seeds of self-consciousness leading to resentment and rebellion, forever. It is caste pride behind this centuries old custom which divides the society even deeper.

> '…I fired off angrily, 'Is it right to go for Salaam?' … The bridegroom goes from door to door at his own wedding. It is awful. The bride grooms of the higher castes don't have to do that…This bride will also go door-to-door after she arrives in Barla.' *Pitaji* has really broken the custom in our house…Pitaji had refused categorically, 'My son would not go Salaaming'… We had told everybody frankly: whosoever wants to give anything must come here and give it.'[20]

This is the new face of Dalit youth who has not only the courage to question humiliating practices and customs of the society but also refused to comply with them.

'Begar' another system against which there is a strong resentment amongst Dalits. A system in which people are captured forcefully to give their labour and do all kind of work like harvesting, tilling, looking after animals, filling water, cleaning the surroundings etc without being paid a single penny. This was not only economic but social exploitation too because only people from Dalit communities were forced to do such works for the simple reason that they were outcastes and financially weak. No upper-caste poor people were ever forced to do 'Begar'. Women of these castes were abused and exploited physically by Savarnas while working in their fields.

Now, young men refused to work without wages and upper-castes realised that they were losing their grip on them. They wanted to maintain their domination without changing anything. Now, due to education and political awareness they speak the language of wage, work, equality and their rights. One can see the resentment against it in all Dalit autobiographies.

> 'This time around, the *basti* folk has refused to work without being paid. We will do it you pay us daily wages, they had said, and that had led to a row.'[21]

There is resentment against injustices done to Dalits irrespective of whether they were educated or not. After working hard in the fields of Savarnas, most of the time they are not given what was promised to them. Young Sheoraj, a Dalit, retaliate against taking sugarcane juice which was licked by a dog, which was given to his blind Baba. He retorts—

> 'I will not take it. It's licked by the dog.' I said. Baba said, 'what are you doing Lambardar? We have given our life to you…and this is what . . .
>
> Next day when he was summoned for the work he said, 'Now you give juice to your animals. We will work somewhere else to feed ourselves.'[22]

One can see that Dalits are prepared to die of hunger rather than working in humiliating conditions. They are not worried about the consequences and raise their voices against injustice.

The word '*Joothan*' means left over food in an eater's plate which would be thrown in the garbage bin. '*Jootha*' means polluted and this word, as mentioned by Arun Prabha Mukherjee, carries the connotation of ritual purity and pollution. Mentioning the practice of Joothan, Balmiki has referred to an incident where his mother revolted against the mighty Savarna Sukhdev Tyagi and threw away the basket full of Joothan. She was not scared of anything and answered him back in anger.

> 'Chowdhuriji, all of your guests have eaten and gone.. please put something on the pattal for my children. They too have awaited for this day.' Sukhdev Singh...said, 'You are taking a basket ful of *Joothan* and on top of that you want food for your children. Don't forget your place, Chuhri. Pick up your basket and get going'. She said to Sukhdev Singh, 'Pick it up and put it inside your house. Feed it to the Baratis tomorrow morning'... Sukhdev Singh had pounced on her to hit her, but my mother had confronted him like a lioness, without being afraid.'[23]

After this incident the author's family stopped taking *Joothan*. Women always played a pivotal role in their resistance against Savarns. They were fearless and a source of strength for the entire family. The larger part of family misfortunes were borne by them courageously without getting being by anything. They were beaten, bruised and abused by their menfolk, exploited by Savarnas outside but had to keep the family going. All most all Dalit women, whether mother of Balmiki Sheoraj or Tulsiram – fought vigorously for their family members and for the betterment, for higher education, to the extent being beaten savagely by the menfolk but would not let their children do the 'dirty job' under any circumstances. These autobiographies are full of such incidences. Balmiki's mother resisted to the wishes of her husband.

> 'Ma and Pitaji had a big fight about this. It had come to blows. Ma had declared unequivocably, 'Omprakash will not do this work.' Pitaji had stormed out angrily.'[24]

Sheoraj's mother resisted all brutalities by her husband for the bright future of her son. She didn't think even once about her own relationship with her husband with whom she was remarried and was taking care of her children.

> "Bhikhari had already broken the slate into tiny pieces. When he wanted to take out the books from my bag and tear them, my mother snatched it from him. He leaped in air and kicked her on her chest, she fell down... She was yelling and abusing him, 'you wretch! Your own son failed so you don't want my Sheoraj to go to the school. This will never happen, you Rascal!"[25]

When women folk were beaten by their husbands savagely, then young ones revolted against their fathers and stood by their mothers. They were the ones, who were witness to the handships faced by their mothers in and outside the house, accompanying them to their work. Women succumb to the physical power of men but their sons were not mute spectators as seen in Tulsiram's '*Murdahiya*', were the author slaps back his father when he is torturing his mother.

> 'Whenever my mother spoke to anyone in the village, my father would start abusing her... one day, when my father picked up a 'faruhi' to beat her, I was standing next to him. I caught his hand and slapped him.'[26]

Dalit women also took active interest with men folk in their fight for justice and equality. They fought against the atrocities of Savarnas and their methods of resistances were unique.

> 'Women used bones of oxen and cows as swords... and some would hold earthen pots full of filth of all sorts including human excreta... and would run towards Brahmins and throw it on them... Scared to hell, these Brahmins would run away. To be touched by it, was considered to be the biggest sin for them.'[27]

Resistance is not only shown by refusing to do a work for Savarnas and in the process being badly abused physically and mentally but also by showing contempt about their belief especially about village pastorals which were mostly written by the elite, portraying Dalits if at all, in a bad light. Most of these pastorals were lyrical and spoke about heavenly life at these villages with picturesque surroundings, full of merry making, abundance of food and water, helpful villagers working in their fields, singing and dancing simultaneously. Therefore, village life was far from any Evil, based on heavenly Good. Valmiki recalls, 'The poetry by Maithali Sharan Gupt that we had been taught in school, 'Ah, how wonderful in this village life'… each word of the poem had proved to be artificial and a lie.'[28] Whereas '*Bechain*' recalls a poetry '*Nandnandani Nadroli*' by a freedom fighter and a Gandhian of his village Raghunath Shashtri.

> 'The entire poetry was based on the Geographical set up of the village. It was high on aesthetics, and full of self praise, the way Charans and Bhats did in the king's court. But they did it because of their dependency on them whereas Shashtriji was a narcist who wrote this. There was not a glimpse of rural fights, the life of Dalit women, illiteracy, untouchability etc.'[29]

Dalit autobiographers shows contempt to all this and write their own village pastorals where they live at the outskirts of a village in the most inhuman conditions, forced to do Begar and denied even basic requirement like clean drinking water. Thus, these autobiographies become an important authentic documents about the life and pathetic conditions faced by Dalits.

If, any Savarna did at all mention Dalits in their writings, it was not done out of any sympathy and there was no sensitivity in the portrayals but for fun and laughter, more out of contempt as Mohan Das Naimishrai points out,

> '…Boom wrote '*Chamarinama*', … not out of any sympathy… and definitely without any sensitivity… His poetries were full of contempt for Dalits. People enjoyed, Dalits felt miserable. Later on, some one

from Dalit Community wrote another poetic collection juxtapose Chamarinama.'[30]

The encounters of these writers with various teachers and peers during their school and college days also throws light on various ways by which they were physically tormented and verbally abused in full public view, without anyone intervening to rescue them. The most prevalent words for them were '*Chuhra, Chuhre ke, Chamari, Chamar Raja, Chamra, Chamraota*'. They were made to sit/stand outside the classroom, sweep floor, sent out of the classrooms on one pretext or other so that they cannot learn their lessons, not letting go to the schools at all, badly beaten by teachers like ruffians. Highly casteist remarks were made by teachers like

> '...*Abey Kala Daroga* stand up straight or else I will make you crooked with my stick... Abey, brother-in-law, progeny of a Chuhra, let me know when you die. You think you are a hero. Today I am going to draw oil from your tresses.'[31]

The incident of Surjan Singh, Balmiki's cousin, brings out the fact that savarnas didn't tolerate the children of Dalits to be superior to them in any way. Dalits are born to be indigent and subservient and how dare they not obey them? Teachers behaved like illiterates with a feudalist mentality and were highly arrogant. Dalit students showed their resistance by asking questions in the class, which were simple but difficult to answer, putting teachers in an awkward situation, directly hitting the caste system and in the process deflating the egoes of Savarnas. The pertinent question 'Why is it this and not that? Bring out the contradictions in the ideology and the behaviour of Savarnas, where words never matches deeds.

Another way to show their resistance was to deconstruct the mythological stories and see through the myths of their oppressors. Here it is important to highlight Gayatri Spivak's famous question, 'can subalterns speak?' A famous incident in the Mahabharata '*Eklavya's Gurudakshina*' can be cited as an example, where

Eklavya a Dalit, is no longer seen as an obedient disciple rather Dronacharya is seen as a treacherous and a biased teacher who tricked his disciple to further his own needs. Modern Dalit youth understands everything and these Eklavyas cannot be tricked into self-mutilation any longer but retorts back to the oppressor.

Dalit School going children showed their resistance against an arrogant teacher by writing their character sketch and laughing at it in groups. One such teacher was Omdatt Tyagi, whose profile, Balmiki and his friends wrote, which was quite popular in those days and people quoted sentences from it.

> 'One day when he and I were feeling frustrated, we wrote a character-sketch of Omdatt Tyagi in English, venting our feelings. Its title was 'A profile of that is'. Once we had written the character sketch, when we started to read it, we were in stitches… Students joined us in our laughter… whole college began to talk about the character sketch.'[32]

The brutal atrocities that Dalits faced everywhere made them aware about their identity. The seeds of discontent were sown and covert resistance gave way to open fights and rebellion which was sometimes on personal level and other times at societal level. Now, Dalits were not a meek and oppressed lot but whenever they were in a position to retaliate, gave a befitting reply to their oppressors. An incident from Balmiki is worth quoting. The author's friend, when chided by Gujjar Chandrapal Verma, began crying, he didn't waite for the consequences and gave him back.

> 'I don't know what happened to me at the moment but I grabbed Chandrapal's neck and pushed him down even though he was twice my height and weight.. kept squirming to free his neck but I did not let go of him…he also begged forgiveness from Shravan Kumar.'[33]

> 'Bechain' mentions an incidence where a young Dalit took revenge for an insult meted out to their old father by first trying to sort out the matter with the

> Zilledar but when they insulted them again, Bakshi, the strongest amongst brothers, broke his head with the stick and he was dead.(p. 77)

Dalits forced by powerful and mighty Savarnas, had no choice but to submit to their whims and do as directed at a given point of time. Small children were also not spared and dragged to the fields as unpaid labourers for hours without any food or water. Young Balmiki was forced to work on the field during examination days but during lunch time it became unbearable for him to take rotis from Tyagis, in a manner people don't even feed their dogs. He resented and ran away to his house.

'Fauza's mother called…She dropped the rotis into my hand from way above, lest her hand touch mine. This gesture was insulting to me. I threw those rotis infront of her and ran towards my home. Fauzaran after me to beat me up but I managed to elude him'.[34]

It was considered improper to ask for money to the Savarnas in lieu of the services offered by Dalits. This was the right of upper-caste to take services without paying money. 'Bechain' retaliates against this practice and beats up the Lodh Rajput without worrying about the consequences. For him, respect is more important than anything Else.

> '… I polished his shoes and Tau asked for money… Lodhi lost his temper and said mockingly… I will get my shoes polished umpteen times without paying single aana…The moment Tau reminded him to mind his language, without loosing a second he slapped Tau and abused him…Tau was partially blind but with all force he threw his shoe on Lodhs head… he was stunned…The moment I heard Taus voice, I ran towards him, took his stick and had beaten Lodh mercilessly.'[35]

The resistance shown by a Dalit and that too blind came as a thunderbolt to Lodh. An insult to Lodh Rajput, beaten by a Dalit in full public view by a Dalit, who are born to be insulted, humiliated, beaten and abused but the entire equation had changed. He was unable to swallow the fact that people doing menial work at footpath too have self-respect and pushed to the corners, even they can retaliate. This is the new wave of young Dalits who will not take any nonsense from anyone and will question their oppressors in their language without any fear. This was the new technique to show resistance to the oppressors because young Dalits are politically conscious and are fully aware of their rights. An excerpt from 'Bechain' proves the point.

> '…I said let Thekedar come and see the work himself then you will understand the difference between your and my work. He got angered by the logic and shouted, '…We are Thekedars and you are a servant. Don't forget and be in your limits'. I was not frightened and answered him with confidence, 'First see my work. What if, I am a labourer? I am getting paid for my work… you can remove me from work but cannot trouble me.'[36]

Dalits are not only an oppressed lot in their native villages but the same kind of humiliation is meted out to them in cities also by either serving them food in separate utensils or change in the behaviour of people once their caste is known. They are also mocked and looked down upon by the way they look and dress.

The so-called elite class forget that the basis of their luxurious life is the hardwork and labour of this economically weaker section of the society. Despite their high education, elite treat Dalits badly. But the Dalit youth is not deterred by the richness and glamour and is ready to fight back for his right. He doesn't keep quiet when subjected to injustices but questions back confidently. When asked to leave the room young Sheoraj replies them.

> '…Your number will come later on. We are here. Go out.' Ma got up whereas I kept standing there for my chance as my legitimate right. 'You have come after us so your turn for the electronic Cremation of the dead would be after us.'[37]

The fight for a Dalit is many fold. He has to resist against the unjust social system and the people who are running it on one hand, and on the other, his own people who practice all sorts of untouchability and are divided in various sects and sub-castes. Economically better off Dalits look down upon their poor cousins who are still doing their ancestral job of leather tanning, working in the fields of savarnas or rearing pigs, which are considered 'dirty' by them. It is not that financially strong Dalits don't understand the sad plight of their brethren but it is their complex and a strong urge to copy high caste norms and in the process carving an identity for themselves, different from the rest of their Dalit community. Eating dead animals, leather work and other such jobs were done out of pure economic reasons rather than anything else. Social and family sanctions were levied against a person who was found doing such things just the way upper caste people did. When the author's Baba was boycotted by the Dalit Community on the above mentioned charge he showed his resistance in strongest possible verbal abuses to his relatives.

> '...You cannot take water from the well.' Baba got up with a jerk furiously and retorted, 'who the hell are you bastards to stop me..have you lost your senses... I have dug this well... on my land... Bastards, you are not Chamar, but fucking bastards, progeny of Thakurs and Babhans... go and dig a well for yourselves and dare you come here... and yes, don't invite us for your rituals.'[38]

Generally Dalit children were named as Kanwa, Phekna, Bigna, Khacheru, Gadchu, Dhingan, Birsa, Piari, etc., because they didn't know that the name is an important part of one's identity. And it has its impact on one's personality. That's why elites often called Dalits by such names so that psychologically they always thought of themselves as small, useless and mean creatures. With education, came understanding and this gave birth to self respect. Dalits resented against calling names by the elite and started a tradition of keeping better sounding names, that arouses a sense of respect in them and a desire to discard those names that sounded stigmatised. Balmikis father called him '*Munshiji*' because Munshis were supposed to be highly learned and respected people. There was a strong urge in Dalits to be learned and respected. Hence, this was also a form of resisting the dominance of Savarnas.

Like social causes there are also strong resistances against religious rituals which are nothing but the by-product of illiteracy, irrational thoughts, and superstitions. Today, modern educated Dalit youth is against any kind of form or ritual worship. They believe in modern science and technology and are dead against practices of various pujas by the older generation. Instead of medical aid provided to a patient the Dalits believed in *ojhas* and *Bhagats* as mentioned by Bechain, which surely didn't yield much result.

> '... I was angry and told amma, 'Is examination done? They ate up the meat and didn't even leave a piece for us... Jija's Money has been squandered away mindlessly.' 'Don't say like this son! Syed Baba, Bengali Baba would be upset. They have accepted, the offerings and your Jija will start speaking from tomorrow'.[39]

Balmiki father was worried that his son might have changed his religion because of his growing estrangement from Chuhra rituals. Not only this, Balmiki didn't succumb to his father's wishes for organising a feast for the community people when he married Chanda. He resisted every pressure whether family or community, and did only what he believed in. The social context makes the author question Hindu caste and society, subsequently challenging it in all possible ways. An opportunity to read and understand Ambedkar's view helped him articulate his views and see the ills of his society.

The Dalits started boycotting Hindu temples after they were humiliated and beaten by Savarnas as reflected in the words of Mohandas Naimishrai:

> '... You the Chamar progeny, you have contaminated me'... There was quietness in the temple but we

> could hear abuses… all temples were for Savarnas… I spat spited on the priest… ' Hell with your temples and your offerings' and came back to my home… after that I never went to temples.'[40]

Whenever, Dalits were verbally abused by Savarnas, they returned it back in the same coins. An incident from '*Bechain*' is worth quoting:

> '…Telin abused us indirectly. Sometimes she would say to her oxen, 'drink water or chamar will cut you into pieces'… sometimes hitting her bitch with a stick, 'why are you sitting ideal like a Chamarin'… Get up or I will break your legs and get you thrown in Chamartoli.' When I grew up, we formed a gang and answered to all her statements like, 'When Telin's oxen dies we will cut it in pieces. See, If it has died or not?'[41]

Language and Aesthetics

Since the personal experiences are the basis of any autobiography therefore, these experiences are considered to be an authentic source to understand the life and times of its author. More than, the external circumstances, it is important to look at the use of the language to understand the inner feelings of an author. The life portrayed in these autobiographies are different from the highly romantic and imaginative writings of the elite class. Form, content, sentence structure and words – all form a part of the aesthetics of literature. With this, another important questions sprouts/sprats up – why and for whom is literature written and how should it be written? There are accepted norms however since the Dalits have a different view of life which is aptly conveyed in their writings therefore the medium in which it is expressed also differs from the aesthetic norms established by the dominant class. It doesn't fit in the elitist notion of writing. It is the language of reality. The language that is spoken by them which is far from the 'cultivated gesture and grammar' of the elite.

Dalit writers in general and particularly autobiographers, have refrained from using the standard language which reflects the arrogant mentality of higher castes. Thus, it has been totally rejected by Dalit writers. They are more familiar with the language of their settlement than the standard language. One can easily see the dialect of the area used in their autobiographies in which writers are more comfortable dialect than the standard form. They are against Sanskritisation of a language. Moreover their experiences and emotions or their anguish and atrocities are voiced in their mother tongue which gives a greater sharpness to their expression.

Epics are literature but Dalits are not portrayed in true colours in them therefore they have reacted bitterly to the religious scriptures of the elite. The images, symbols, metaphors and similies used by Dalits are those that are appropriate for relating experiences. If at all religious symbols are used in their writings the main idea is to 'deconstruct' them for a new meaning and purpose.

Dalit writers use language consciously so that their pain, anguish, resentment can be communicated effectively. Generally, metaphors and similies are chosen from their surroundings, not from Hindu mythologies to resist the hegemony of elite. Exceptions are there. To describe his mothers anger after being humiliated by Sukhdev Tyagi, Balmiki uses the metaphor of Goddess Durga to describe his mothers heroic action and anger.

The words used by Dalit authors are not standards words used by elite. They have a vocabulary of their own based on their work culture, objects, situations and activities they do and contains words from dialects which are not considered standard by elite.

Even, the choice of the titles of autobiographies like '*Joothan*', '*Murdahiya*', '*Apne-Apne Pinjare*' or '*Mera Bachpan Mere Kandhon Par*'– reflect a strong resistance to the formalist – Elitist notion and in contrast generate pain, humiliation and poverty of Dalits. These words have negative connotations.

The issue of resistance should be seen from both angles. The discriminator and the discriminated. The whole struggle of Dalit movement is based on the issue of acceptance of Dalits by higher caste but the acceptance is not there. This can be traced in the History of Dalit movement. Dr Ambedkar was the first person who understood it fully and fought for the rights of Dalits as a 'human being'. His first agitation was for drinking water from the same tank from which Savarnas drank and second agitation was for entry in the Kala Ram temple. It was a fight against inequality, injustice and discrimination.

Although, caste is relevant today, the power attached to this is under attack in a democratic set up. Traditionally the way these caste groups interacted with each other has been shaken and because of the change in the power dynamics, they view each other with suspicion, hated and fear.

A majority of lower caste groups are economically disadvantaged but are juxtaposed with a highly resourceful dominant caste. The highly resourceful dominant caste show strong resistance to the demands of Dalits for inter-community relations and equality. Savarnas are used to seeing them as subservient workers. With hard work and consequent changes in their life style, Dalits are an eyesore for them. With the changing time the fiefdoms of elites are dwindling and their inflated sense of ego is deflated by high self-esteem in the new generation of educated Dalits. The legitimate protection of rights are perceived as intolerable, disrespectful and rebellion. It is taken as a challenge and is remembered until an opportunity arises to teach them a "lesson" which is often a reason for caste violence. It is the most brutal form of resistance. Another reason of resistance is their own dominant caste origin where they are conditioned in such a way that they start thinking that they are born to rule. It is deeply engraved in the minds of savarnas.

The socio-economic changes in our society have not made expected changes in the existing social fabric. Social mobility or any effort in this direction remain closed to Dalits. An urge for changes in the upward direction in the social system receive a greater amount of resistance by the Savarnas because for them any decline in social distance is not normative in social structure, hence non-acceptable. The 'status-lines'[42] of the Savarnas are under constant threat by Dalit at both individual as well as societal level because of higher mobility and new economic openings. Therefore, there is a very strong resistance on the part of Savarnas to defend their vested interest in the 'status privilege scheme'[43] within the given system. The changing position of Dalits is the main cause of high resistance from Savarnas.

The defying of age old caste system and other restrictions are seen as challenge to the social dominance and autonomy of Savarnas by Dalits. The high aspirations and expectations have made Dalits progressive but the Savarnas are still 'locked in caste customs and prejudices'[44] or 'trapped by traditions',[45] treat Dalits inhumanly and contemptuously.

Language is the major tool for the Savarnas to show their resistance to changes that are significant in Dalits, primarily education. It has brought a revolutionary transformation in their lives. They are highly conscious of themselves and their self-esteem is very high which is difficult for the Savarnas to digest. The arrogances and the jealousies of the elite can be seen in the kind of language they use for them. It is also an effective way to weaken them psychologically so that they can never ever dream to hold their head high. An example from '*Joothan*' will prove it.

' One day the headmaster Kaliram called me… asked, 'Abey, What is your name ? 'Omprakash',…. '*Chuhre ka*?'… All right… sweep the whole school clean as a mirror. It is, afterall, your family occupation'. The third day I went to the class and sat down quietly. After a few minutes the headmasters loud thundering was heard, '*Abey Chuhre ke*, motherfucker, where are you hiding… your mother… .[46]

This is not the language of the Headmaster of a school but of a ruffian. One can see the prejudices in this casteist remark. Abusing is nothing else but a form of verbal resistance. 'They' are meant for the menial jobs. How dare they think of studying?

> '... Go sweep the whole playground... otherwise I will shore chillies up your arse and throw you out of the school.'[47]

The frustration of Savarnas are well reflected in these lines who are helpless to do anything to stop Dalits. The only thing the Savarnas can boast of is their caste tag.

> 'The Chuhras' progency also study in the school?' She said in surprise. 'Howsoever much you study...you will still remain a Chuhra.' She said, taking out her frustration, and went in.'[48]

'Begar' was a system in which poor, mostly Dalits had to work for rich and mighty; for Savarnas, without demanding any single penny as wage. This was another way to show their power and teach a lesson to Dalits.

> 'The Tagas had realised that we were getting out of their control. Therefore, the moment wages were demanded, they would get hopping mad. They were looking for a way to maintain their domination without changing anything. They had taken the help of the chief constable of Purkazi police station who belonged to their caste. He was looking for an occasion, which had suddenly fallen into his hand.'[49]

Like 'Begar', 'Salaam' was another painful system in which the bridegroom had to endure terrible humiliation.

> 'It is caste pride that is behind this century old custom. The deep chasm that divides the society is made even deeper by this custom. It is a conspiracy to trap us in the whirlpool of inferiority.'[50]

To prevent the upsurge of Dalits, Savarnas show their resistance through more attacking forms of discrimination which involves treating them inhumanly so that social identity becomes stronger and in the process crushes the self-esteem of the people on the margin. On one hand the Savarnas use these strategies in the form of social comparisons and on another the confrontations in order to strengthen their group identity to keep Dalits out of social relations because of growing awareness in them.

Caste has functioned, in the past and today, to keep the untouchables and the poor of other castes, who might be equally exploited from uniting for the purpose of seeking improvement in their lives. The position of Dalits in a village is subject to the political manipulations of members of the elite, who often try to keep political and economic control by dividing untouchables among themselves in order to maintain traditional barriers between them.

Especially, those Dalits who have some education and work experience outside the village are now beginning to see that they might be able to gain some political power by virtue of their numbers. So an outcome of this, end up political parties take advantage for their vested interest.

A society has to be based on the mutual understanding, respect and cooperation of all, if at all it wants to move forward. Inequalities in human relationship based on birth or religious beliefs, which society perpetrates, arrests the flow of life with the long subjugated and down trodden sections of the society in this case in Dalits who believe that getting their due place in the society, their lives will regain its dynamism. The ultimate moving force in our lives is the human spirit. Whenever it is in shackles due to stagnancy then it has to be destroyed and rebuilt to ensure its free movement.

Widespread education brought transformation in the lives of people. It made them conscious about the rights of people such as equality, liberty, fraternity and justice guaranteed by the Indian constitution. But, the inequalitable system, throttled the voice of the 'weak' which led to dissatisfaction, resistance and finally revolt against this inhuman, barbaric and tyrannical system of caste.

Armed with high education and best degrees, Dalit youth fully understood the importance of struggle. There is tremendous awakening in Dalit society due to education. With the spread of formal education, some changes have been observed in their choice of occupation. The educated and the semi-educated youths show reluctance to work as labourers/bonded labourers or do the work specifically meant to be done by 'their caste'. The new generation of Dalits strongly resist against doing such jobs which are looked down upon by the elites. Most of them have given up the job of scavengers, carrying dead animals tannery etc. and strongly feel that they can achieve higher status and prestige by being employed in government jobs. If this is not possible, then they are ready to do any 'clean' job which does not contaminate them.

It is clear that there are various levels of protest some subtle and some overt, in the Dalit literary genres and forms. Sometimes it is in the form of protest against the socio-political organisations and Institutions. At times it is resurgent and generates vigorous activity. The system itself is so stifling, that it doesn't allow a person to breathe, to take a pause or to think and react to a situations in a rational way. At times the resistance is in the form of a monologue or in an inner dialogue with oneself. At other times, it assumes the form of a satire, cynism towards the double standard of the four tier Brahmanical society. The out-burst of a Dalit is not just an emotional one but much more than that. It is a sense of loss of everything that he stands for. It is a do or die situation for him, a question mark on his identity, his presence and his being. Today Dalit literature is not limited to merely emotional purposes and appeal. It shuns sentimentality and is robust in its range, temper and meaning.

The anger of the Dalit Community, their resolve to fight against all kinds of exploitation and a total refusal to bear any kind of burden of the elite is clearly seen and felt in these writings. One can see the new generation of Dalits who are politically articulate, organised, highly conscious and vocal in assertion of their rights. The questions about caste asked are more analytical, logical and scientific in their temperament and rejects the category as the sole identity of human beings.

Dalit literature, constructs a new wave in Hindi literature in particular and Indian literature in general. These literary works show that a system based on such inhuman, tyrannical exploitation is bound to collapse. The society can no longer afford to be indifferent to the repression of the people on the margins, who are considered untouchable on the basis of their birth. The new stream of Dalit literature is not apologetic but assertive and directly questions the people who are on the top of the caste Pyramid and perpetuates its very existence and continuity.

'The journey of our slavery
begins from your birth
and it would end
With your end.'[51]

References

1. *Towards an Aesthetics of Dalit Literature*, (Tr.) Alok Mukherjee Orient Longmna, Hyderabad, India, 2004.
2. *Dalit Politics and Literature*, Pradeep Kumar Sharma, Shilpa Publication, Delhi, 2011.
3. *The Language of Autobiography*, John Strruck, Cambridge University Press, Cambridge, 1993.
4. *Joothan : Atma Katha*, Omprakash Valmiki, Radhakrishna Prakashan Pvt. Ltd., New Delhi, 1997.
5. *Mera Bachpan Mere Kandhon Par*, Sheoraj Singh 'Bechain', Vani Prakashan, New Delhi, 2009.
6. *Murdahiya,* Tulsiram, Rajkamal Prakashan, New Delhi, 2010.
7. *Apne-Apne Pinjare*, Mohandas Naimishrai, Vani Prakashan, New Delhi, 1995.
8. *Identity in Asian Literature*, (ed.) Lisbeth Littrup, Curzon Press Ltd., Survey, 1996.
9. *Joothan, A Dalit Life*, (Tr.) Arun Prabha Mukherjee, Samya, Kolkata, 2010.
10. *Dalit Asmita* (Quarterly Magazine) published by Indian Institute of Dalit Studies (IIDS) 2011-2012 editions.
11. *Why I am not a Hindu*, Kancha Ilaiah, Samya, Kolkata, 1996.

9

Marginalising of the Tribals: Literature as Resistance

Mahasveta Devi and *Dinesh Misra*

Literature is the eternal voice of resistance to injustice and oppression. The disadvantaged sections of the society, who were kept out or pushed out of the path of development, have remained on the margin and their life has become an unending saga of pain and misery. They are rendered voiceless by the sheer immensity of the unfairness and mischief they are subjected to. But conscientious writers have taken up cudgels on their behalf and have exposed the exploitation and the criminal conspiracy against the tribal people.

Of course, Indian society has come a long way since the hoary times when *rishis* and *munis* dominated the scene with their spiritual precepts and ascetic ways. The common people, as well as the ruling classes, paid obeisance to them and tried to follow the path shown by them. The *rishis* preached lessons of humanity, fraternity and happiness for all. (*Sarve bhavantu sukhina sarve santu niramaya.*) Everyone was to be happy and without fear. A divine message indeed!

But as time marched on, things began to change — a change in the social and economic spheres of the society. It was a downward turn. And it so happened that influential segments of the society made remarkable progress and their segment of the society developed. But, a sizeable chunk of humanity, gradually, was left out of the mainstream. In large numbers, the deprived sections had to move into the forest for survival and sustenance. The process was grim and painful, but somehow, they lived on. In due course, they were almost forgotten by the society at large, the so-called mainstream, and they were given the label of tribes. Instead of citizens, they became tribals.

However, the tribals came to an understanding with their destiny and began to live in consonance with conditions of the wild forest. In small settlements, they began to live in the forest and found some means to sustain themselves. They developed an instinct for survival and joyful satisfaction in the way they had to live in the wild. In spite of immense trials and tribulations, as well as an ever-present threat of life they acquired an almost idyllic existence.

But with the advent of the so-called economic growth and industrialisation, things began to change for the worse, so far as the tribals were concerned. Cunning people, in connivance with the state authority, came to realise that most of the forests were rich in minerals, fuel oils and many other valuable things. So, plans were chalked out, and a ceaseless campaign began for numerous projects of mining, drilling and umpteen avaricious activities in the forests. The tribals were uprooted from their own soil where they had been living for centuries.

Globalisation resulted in more money pouring in for mining, oil drilling and many other disruptive enterprises. An ever-growing number of industries usurped thousands of acres of precious land which had traditionally, and always, belonged to the tribal people, now ruthlessly being thrown out of their habitat, in a most unjust and inhuman way.

Literature could not remain a silent spectator to this callous phenomenon of injustice and tyranny. A number of authors, in different Indian languages, observed the injustice that was being meted out to the tribal people. They had a close look at the ugly scenario and found that tribals, the *adivasis*, were benumbed with shock and fear. As writers, they considered it their duty to oppose this injustice and resist the greed of the industrialists and oppression of the state. They had to become voice of the voiceless.

One such voice, strong and clear, firm and fearless, is that of Mahasveta Devi, the great Bangla writer, the doyen of Indian authors and intellectuals, who has extended all support to the hapless tribal communities. In novel after novel, in story after story, Mahasveta Devi uncovers the horrible devastation of tribal communities in the name of progress and development. She understands the pain of the marginalised people. She is aware of the agony of the people whose lives have been turned into a nightmare by the despicable conspiracy of greedy industrialists, corrupt bureaucracy and scheming politicians. Mahasveta Devi describes and condemns the cruel exploitation of the tribal people by industrialists and their cohorts. Not only that, she also criticizes and deplores the so-called progressives and the mischievous party cadre for confusing the issues and obstructing unity of the struggling tribals.

In her novel *Chotti Munda and His Arrow*, she depicts the suffering of tribals, as time rolls by. Even after India became free, the process has not stopped or softened. Instead, things have got much worse. Mahasveta Devi visited the tribal regions and saw with her own eyes what horrors were being committed in the guise of development. She observed 'the criminalisation of politics that let the lumpen loose in the tribal belts.' What *Chotti Munda* depicts is the resistance to all this, a continuing struggle. Earlier, there was the rebellion of Birsa Munda, from 1895 to 1900. Even before that, there had been many tribal rebellions.

Yet after each rebellion — always related to land and labour — they were evicted from their traditional home. Mahasveta Devi says that the tribals did not find anyone writing about them and they did not have a script. So, they composed the stream of events into songs. Their history is like a big flowing river going somewhere but having a lot of obstacles and hindrances. In her novel *Pterodactyl*, Mahasveta Devi produces a vivid picture of the tribal consciousness, their culture, the excruciating oppression, and their struggle for human dignity. *Pterodactyl* is a brilliant mix of realism and fantasy which gives an expression to the physical torments the tribal people have to undergo. It also highlights new dimensions of their spiritual and cultural awareness. It cautions them about their tasks and responsibilities towards their own people as well as towards the enlightened Indian opinion of the mainstream.

She says : I wrote in *Pterodactyl* that the tribal world was like a continent handed over to us and we never tried to explore it, know its mysteries; we only destroyed it. It's very difficult to re-knit that entire experience without knowing what their potentiality was, how much they have to give.

About *Chotti Munda,* Mahasveta Devi found that Birsa Munda's uprising did not die with Birsa. And so, through the figure of Dhani, she wanted to say that there had to be a magic arrow, not magic in the narrow sense, but an arrow that Dhani Munda wanted to hand over. This arrow was a symbol for the person who would carry on that continuity. *Chotti Munda* is an emblem of that.

What Mahasveta Devi does is to read between the unwritten lines of the tribals' story, as Gayatri Chakravorty Spivak puts it. *Chotti Munda* is a symbol or representation of tribal aspiration. That is why, the beginning of the book, Mahasveta Devi says, opens into the mythic ancestor — continuity placed within an open frame at both ends.

Mahasveta Devi lived with tribals for long periods because she believes that, if we have to know about tribals, we have to go back in tradition, in oral tradition, re-read something that is not written.

Mahasveta Devi says : The tragedy of India, when it became independent, was not introducing thorough land reforms. A basically feudal land system was allowed to stay. A feudal land system can only nurture and sustain a feudal value system. A feudal system is anti-women, anti-poor people, against the toiling people. It is the landowners who formed the ministry, and became the rulers of the country. Why should they do anything else?

The novel *Pterodactyl* was published a few years after *Chotti Munda*. It is much more tragic and pessimistic. But Mahasveta Devi thinks that her novels, in spite of the depiction of misery, suffering and struggle, still have an element of hope. For example, her earlier novel *Aranyer Adhikar* indicated a way out of the gloom. In *Pterodactyl* also, according to Mahasveta Devi, there is hope, because they are saying at the end that they will plant thorns and eat the tuber. They are learning to cope with the modern, they are not accepting defeat, they will not be crushed. They know that charity will come and go, that the government will do nothing or almost nothing. But they are not accepting defeat. *Pterodactyl* is the crux of her tribal experience. She does not see the tribals as defeated and crushed.

Pterodactyl is half human, half bird; creature which incarnates in the form of the spirit of forefathers of the tribesmen. It associates the struggle of that whole tribal community against exploitation and oppression with a new myth. This novel narrates a story in the background of Pirtha, an imaginary hillock area in Madhya Pradesh. The novel tells the reader about the all-devouring and voracious capitalist onslaught and the age-old equitable cultural and social traditions, and the confrontation of two life styles and two types of life values. The whole plot is finely balanced between the extraordinary and the ordinary, between the eternal and the modern; so much so that the reader travels through that human tragedy from the spiritual to the physical. It tells us not only about the present, but the future is also laid bare before our eyes.

Mahasveta Devi has a penchant for recreating significant periods of history. The characters or the individuals, she picks up from that period, pass through remarkable events in which they continue to grow and evolve by interacting with the historical process. In *Chotti Munda and His Arrow*, happening in the beginning of the 20th century and continuing through the first seven decades — during that period what happened to one of the tribes of eastern India, the *Mundas*, is depicted in the novel.

Mahasveta Devi is a chronicler. She is sensitive to the nuances of oral narratives as well as speech, jumbled up with words from different sources. Her works are full of lyrical moments that highlight dramatic high-points as well as awesome details of treachery and perfidy of the exploiters of tribal communities.

When Mahasveta Devi wrote *Aranyer Adhikar*, she recreated the character of Birsa Munda, who led the tribal revolt. In her narrative, history and folklore and fiction are all mixed up, to create a state of emotional high. This affects the readers' conscience. It highlights the spirit and passions of the time. She does not indulge in sentimental romanticisation. In her own words, Mahasveta Devi explains : "Once I became a professional writer, I felt increasingly that a writer should document his own time and history. The socio-economic history of human development has always fascinated me."

The tribals have suffered marginality and its inevitable deprivations for a long time. Literature has been a witness to it, but not a dumb witness. Writers like Mahasveta Devi in their novels, short stories and prose writings have exposed villainy of the profit-mongering industrial and mining corporates, in connivance with the ruling classes. Mahasveta Devi is firmly of the view that the forests belong to the forest-dwellers, the tribal communities. They must not be, and can not be, ousted from their own land and environment, just to satisfy the ambitions of some profiteers with an insatiable greed.

Thus, literature proves to be, not only the portrayer of marginality, but also a saviour of the down trodden people and also of the human values.

10

Mapping the Self, Mapping Dalithood: Namdeo Dhasal–Poet and Panther

Ms. Kalyanee Rajan

"I am proud to be one of the voices raised on behalf of millions of exploited Dalits."

Arjun Dangle[1], Introduction to 'The Poisoned Bread'.

In this paper, I propose to examine the poetry of Namdeo Dhasal, also a Dalit Panther, as an exercise of mapping the "self" inextricably intertwined with the process of mapping dalithood. I shall begin by briefly touching upon the background of Dalit writing— its origin, concrete articulation and contemporary situation as shaped by various influences and phases in Dalit Literature.

SECTION I

Dalit Literature as a clearly defined category begins to emerge in the twentieth century. It is a literary movement emerging from a sustained struggle by Dalit writers to bring about a humane restructuring of the society and a radical social change. The term 'Dalit' was introduced officially only in 1958 in the first conference of the Maharashtra Dalit Sahitya Sangha in Bombay. Etymologically, the term 'Dalit' is derived from the Sanskrit root 'dal' that means burst, broken or torn asunder, scattered, crushed and destroyed (V.S. Apte[2]). Scholars are of the view that the mythological text called '*Manusmriti*' in the Indian history forced a complete erasure or silencing of any favourable representation of Dalit reality and life-style in the domain of everyday socio-cultural paradigms, let alone the sphere of literary epistemology.

Datta Bhagat[3] elucidates further about the origins of the word 'Dalit' which according to him refers to a broad underclass of people – not just the untouchables of Hindu Caste communities but also other oppressed communities including the *adivasis*, the poor, the labourers and so on. At the same time, Bhagat clarifies that this broad-spectrum definition is not implied by the term 'Dalit' as used in Dalit Literature. Here, 'Dalit' refers to the outcaste communities of India that were discriminated against on the basis of birth. Dalit Literature in its present form registers protest; uncovers hypocritical double standards of behaviour among Caste followers; acquaints readers with and expresses anger at the inhuman treatment experienced by such communities. It follows then that Dalit writing aims at eradicating social discrimination to usher in an egalitarian society upholding democratic ideals. Arjun Dangle[4], one of the foremost Dalit writers describes Dalit Literature as ...' marked by *revolt* and *negativism*, since it is closely associated with *hopes for freedom* of a group of people who, as *untouchables*, are victims of *social, economic and cultural inequality*.' (Emphasis added).

To situate Dalit writing in its historical context: two chief visionaries from Maharashtra – Mahatma Jyotiba Phule (1828-1890) and Dr Bheemrao Ramji Ambedkar (1891-1956), anchor the entire ideology of the 'Dalit'. Jyotiba Phule, a reformist and staunch critic of the Hindu caste system, advocated equal rights and education for women and the *untouchable* community. He critiqued the exploitative policies of caste Hindus through his *Satya Shodhak Samaj* founded in 1873 in Pune. It would be pertinent here to note that Phule himself belonged to the *mali* caste and founded the *Samaj* along with four or five associates from not-so-elevated castes.

Ambedkar's influence on Dalit writing has been more extensive and widely recognised. He became the primary impetus for the self-conscious, socially critical and political art of the Dalit writers. In 1926, he mobilised his supporters to break the ban on *untouchables* from drinking water from the town tank in Mahad in the Konkan. The Mahad Satyagraha (1927) often called the 'first untouchable liberation struggle' concluded with the public burning of the *Manusmriti* – sending shockwaves in the upper caste Hindu society. For Ambedkar[5], Mahatma Gandhi was a defender of Caste system. In his essay "Gandhism: The Doom of Untouchables" he interrogated Gandhism and its emancipatory rhetoric, perhaps hinting at Gandhi's envisioning of the Dalits as '*Harijans*'. Ambedkar quotes Gandhi "I gave *support to Caste* because it stands for restraint." and further, "The best remedy is that ... we may *reproduce the old system* of four Varnas." (Emphasis added). In the same vein, Ambedkar accuses Gandhi of neglecting the depressed classes saying, "Mr. Gandhi does not wish to hurt the propertied class." Ambedkar also charges Gandhism as being unsuitable to a society adhering to democratic ideals in both its social and economic outlook. Nicholas B. Dirks[6] has described this fundamental ideological confrontation between Gandhi and Ambedkar in an essay 'The Reformation of Caste' in his significant book, "Castes of Mind". In his fortnightly magazine 'Bahiskrit Bharat' (started on April 4, 1927), Ambedkar defines Dalithood as "a kind of *life condition* that characterises the *exploitation, suppression and marginalisation* of the lower castes by the social, economic, cultural and political *domination of the upper caste* Brahminical order" (Emphasis added).

Mahatma Gandhi's well calculated intervention in the ongoing struggle against *untouchability* served to complicate the picture further. He saw the need for reform in the hardcore casteist society before the people could be united in the struggle for Indian independence. However, he was completely at odds with Ambedkar's ideas for Dalit struggle. His ambitious all-inclusive coinage '*Harijan*' meaning people of God was considered revolting and patronising by the Dalits themselves instead of emancipatory and respectful (Veena Deo[7]).

Writers such as Baburao Bagul, Bandhu Madhav, Waman Nimbalkar, Shankarrao Kharat, Daya Pawar, Yadavrao Gungurde, Raja Dhale, Yogendra Meshram, Arjun Dangle, Prakash Jadhav, Chokha Kamble to name a few, marked the first phase of Dalit writing. Namdeo Dhasal's first collection of poems Golpitha (1972) and the subsequent political movement of the Dalit Panther, which served to reformulate and reorient the stream of Dalit Literature, inaugurated the second and more revolutionary phase of Dalit writing. Veena Deo[8] makes an important observation here; she thinks that many Dalit writers see the connection between the struggle of Dalits for their rights and literary output as a parallel struggle to that of the Black communities in the U.S. Hence their immense respect for Black Literature and emulation of Martin Luther King.

Within, the larger trend of Dalit literary assertion and expression, Autobiography is one of the most central and popular genres. On one hand, it is the primary vehicle of expression of Dalit writers to articulate their suppressed voices. This makes the Autobiography constitute a dynamic space through which the Dalits can for the first time, bring out a 'rupture' in the elite literary public sphere. On the other hand, the form of Autobiography has gone beyond being a mere launch pad for participation of Dalits in the mainstream public debate. It has over time become a standard 'leit motif' and inspiring force in Dalit expression, constituting the individuality of the Dalit writer as possessing a potent subjectivity. It also serves to effectively portray the so-called 'victimised' and 'eternally stigmatised' Dalit community.

S.P. Punalekar[9] remarks, "Dalit writers themselves are either victims or witness to social inequalities and violence. Some have direct or indirect links with... Dalits. A few among them are staunch social activists and (they) use literature to propagate their views on Dalit identity and the prevailing social consciousness." Taking cue from this remark, it can be deduced that by using Autobiography as a potent tool, the Dalit writer embarks on a manifold agenda. Firstly, s/he exposes the harsh realities of Dalit existence and the continuation of Caste-based discrimination. Secondly, it serves to highlight the fragile and tenuously constructed Dalit self-hood, which has to negotiate constantly with systematic disenfranchisement and social subordination as well as material disprivilaging of the Dalits even in the post independence era. Finally, Autobiography provides an apt platform for language to fashion itself as a site of creation of entirely new identities. There is a persistent underlying quest in Dalit literature for creating a radically altered public space modelled on truly democratic ideals. Dalit Autobiography also reveals varied facets of the Dalit movement, argues Dalit literary ace Arjun Dangle[10]. For him, Dalit Autobiography depicts a struggle for identity and survival; the complicated "emotional universe of a Dalit's life; the man-woman relationship; an existence crushed under the wheels of village life; the experiencing of humiliation and atrocities; *at times, abject submission, at other times, rebellion*." (emphasis added). It is significant to note here that Dalit Autobiography constantly invokes multiple subjectivities where the individual marker 'I' connects smoothly yet subtly to the communal marker 'we', usually encompassing the entire community within its folds.

As an aside, I would like to mention here that Dalit women have also been contributing to literature and poetry since 1930's. Dalit women writers have predominantly used Autobiographical writing and have experimented extensively within the genre. Hence, they require a wider and separate historical evaluation of their role and the complexity arising due to gender, which again problematises the issue. Shantabai Kamble, Meena Gajbhiye, Surekha Bhagat, Hira Bansode, Jyoti Lanjewar, Meenakshi Mun, Baby Kamble and Urmila Pawar are some names that must be mentioned in this context, suggesting a steadily growing concert of voices.

SECTION II

In this section, using Dilip Chitre's introduction as the primary source[11], I would attempt to provide a brief biographical history of the person Namdeo Dhasal, one of the pioneer architects of the Dalit Panther Movement. Namdeo Laxman Dhasal was born in Pur-Karnesar, a small village near Poona, to Laxman Dhasal and his second wife, Salubai on February 15, 1949. Born a *mahar* and therefore branded an *untouchable*, Namdeo was aware of the stigma it carried even as a child. In the 1950's, when he came to Mumbai as an immigrant, he was transplanted to Mumbai's dark underbelly- the red-light area of *Dhor Chawl* in Golpitha. Leaving his land and farming, Laxman Dhasal became a wage earning labourer carrying animal carcasses for a Muslim butcher. The congenitally stigmatised identity of a *mahar,* however, ensured that he remained an *untouchable* as well as a loathed meat-eater in the eyes of the caste Hindus. Dilip Chitre recounts for us that Dhasal grew up in a claustrophobic world peopled by prostitutes and pimps, transgenders, loan sharks, corrupt cops, drug addicts, petty criminals, street urchins, sexually transmitted diseases, quacks and physicians, gangsters, singers and mujra dancers, coolies, immigrant labourers, liquor vendors, food vendors et cetera, to sum up, a motley of people who spiced the streets and their life (as told to Dilip Chitre[12]). To cite a recent example, Danny Boyle's Oscar winning film, *Slumdog Millionaire* (2009) offers a slice of this dark reality of Mumbai. Thus, the ideas of pollution and contamination, which are shocking to any educated person, are brought forward convincingly by Dhasal in his incomparable style.

He married Malika Amar Sheikh, the daughter of legendary communist poet Amar Sheikh. Dhasal was an ardent follower of Ambedkar and Ram Manohar Lohia. He said in an interview, "I became a socialist. However, whatever I did, my foundation was Ambedkar's vision." In his book *Dalit Personal Narratives* (2010)[13], Raj Kumar talks of how Dhasal infused the term *Dalit* with a leftist vision to include other economically depressed classes such as STs, Neo-Buddhists, landless labourers apart from the originally intended Scheduled castes, which is a very crucial intervention in social terms.

Dhasal was very conscious of his origins and identity as a Dalit. His first collection of poems, Golpitha, which was published in 1972, quite interestingly, by a right wing Brahmin activist Narayan Athavale, burst like a bombshell in the placid precincts of Marathi Poetry. In the same year, on July 9, 1972, he proceeded to cofound the Dalit Panther with J.V.Pawar, Arjun Dangle and Raja Dhale. The Dalit Panther Manifesto of 1973 declared it's agenda of fighting for the liberation of Indian Dalits through a "complete revolution"[14]. It was launched along the lines of the Black Panther movement of Oakland fighting for Black American Liberation in the United States of America. Studies reveal that though it did not last long, the Dalit Panther movement was considered politically significant by a large section of people[15].

By 1982, ideological disputes began to crack the Dalit Panthers and the movement gradually lost its momentum. In keeping with his controversial style, Dhasal created a furore by appearing on the dais of the right wing *Shiv Sena* in 1997 to which the Dalit Panther had been violently opposed to for decades[16]. In 2006 again, he appeared on the RSS platform, very much in keeping with his conflicting views about politics. This Paper however looks at the early poetry of Dhasal and tries to bring to fore the sustained revivalism of a subversive Dalit humanity in his poetry.

Tapan Basu astutely observes that Dhasal writes in a fluid mix of dialects in Marathi and a certain 'roughness' of linguistic idiom pervades his poetry which baffled the traditional Marathi Literati. His work is linguistically too complex and deeply embedded in its own ethos. Vijay Tendulkar, the celebrated Marathi playwright who wrote the introduction to the first edition of *Golpitha*, was forced to admit that this 'general incomprehensibility' of language in Dhasal, which is like inverted snobbery, is the strength of *Golpitha*.

In *Golpitha*, one can see how he inverts Classical Sanskrit Aesthetic Theory in his poetry by pitting a nauseous feeling against a combination of the *rasas,* the *sringara* or the erotic, the *adbhuta* or the marvelous, the *raudra* or the furious and so on, i.e. all the feelings on which most literature is based. In a poem "Cruelty", he shockingly declares, "I am a venereal sore in the private part of language..." The graphic imagery of Dhasal's poetry is found very often to vividly picturise gross things: the contents of sewers and stagnant pools of waters for instance which confront the onlooker by way of both the crucial senses of sight and smell. The senses are, hence, as if besieged by the quantum of tangibly palpable filth and stink, which is a part of the conventional image of the 'loathsome' *untouchable* in the perception of the chaste and *touchable* caste Hindus.

SECTION III

In this final section, I would attempt to analyse the mapping of the "self" and "dalithood" by Dhasal through a close reading of his poems. Dhasal himself said, "*Golpitha* was an attempt to interpret myself. What is poetry but autobiography anyway?" His personal experience of being a *mahar* becomes the central preoccupation of Dhasal as a creative writer rendering his poems in a language that defies penetration beyond a certain point even to erudite native Maharashtrians like Tendulkar and Dilip Chitre. They are forced to admit that Dhasal's poems defy linear denouement and literal translation due to his technique of free association and his spontaneous contextual leaps.

For K. Satchidanandan[17], the enormous corpus of aggressive Dalit poetry in Marathi constitutes a "...dissenting collective, another *alternative nationhood*, that articulates the *silent anguish and indignation* of the so called '*untouchables'* relegated to the bottom of the Caste hierarchy for more than thirty centuries." (Emphasis added). Furthermore, the diction of poets like Dhasal not only rejects the norms set by brahminic poetics and throws overboard classical values like propriety, balance, restraint and understatement but is at the same time deliberately subversive, challenging the middle class norms of decency.

Tapan Basu[18] in his essay "*Narratives of sufferings; Dalit perspectives*" notes that Dhasal's use of colloquial language of the lower castes '...struck a jarring note in the existing symphony of Marathi literature.' Dhasal infuses the local slang of the red light district of *Golpitha* with standard mainstream Marathi violating the literary tastes of the reader to force him to an acknowledgement and understanding of the convulsive reality of Dalit existence.

As discussed earlier, S. P. Punalekar[19] remarks, "Dalit writers themselves are either victims or witness to social inequalities and violence." It can be safely deduced that the venom that Dhasal spews out in his poetry stems from both his personal experiences as well as his countess associations in his community. The cover of *Golpitha* carried a 'Performa of the Municipal Corporation' of greater Bombay's venereal diseases clinic, highlighting the profane *untouchable* world that he inhabited, the dirty, unsanitary and diseased world, which is an integral part of Dalit existence. Interestingly, Dhasal wrote poetry easily, as he candidly admits himself[20], "When I was a taxi driver, I went to a particular eatery to have food. I would (simply) sit there and write what I had on my mind." Dhasal never writes in English. All his works are available as translations by various people, mostly either by Dilip Chitre or Jayant Karve.

For Aniket Jaaware[21], in the essay "Eating and Eating with the Dalit: A re-consideration touching upon Marathi poetry", the 'abandonment with which the diction of poetry is explored, the traditional registers deployed to romantic or ironic effect, the arbitrary or arbitrary-seeming divisions of line and the frequent mixture of registers' are characteristic markers of Dhasal's poetry. Jaaware further proposes that caustic poetic outburst like Dhasal's belongs to the second basic mould of Dalit speech- that of protest or revolution; the first being the mould of 'entreaty' as in the first nascent phase of Dalit poetry while the third mould which aptly describes the third and present phase is the mould of 'empty rhetorical gesture'. Jaaware suggests that in the third phase, the ethical strength of the Dalit poet's voice has dissipated itself either into a diminished, minimal speech, or into an empty rhetorical gesture towards ethics with the poet reflecting no more on social conditions but their literary expression turning Dalit poetry into a 'tradition of production, circulation and consumption'. It will be interesting to explore this third mould with respect to Dhasal's later works and his shifting political allegiances elsewhere.

Veena Deo[22] in her essay "Dalit literature in Marathi" dwells at length on the origin and development of Dalit literature. She proceeds to make useful observations on Dhasal's poetic oeuvre. She argues that his poetry offers an open challenge to the elite and the middle class reader alike. She begins by comparing Dhasal to the doyen of Dalit literature Baburao Bagul's generation. Though, they challenged many literary conventions, the writers were still riveted to 'good' writing, which followed certain conventions of genre and literary language. Dhasal on the other hand, is 'self-consciously iconoclastic' and is known to use vocabulary deliberately to ruffle the literary tastes of the reader. He tends to specifically force the reader into an acknowledgement that literary language can not be allowed to distance readers from 'horrific' human experiences and man's 'inhumanity' to man. For instance, he does not 'romanticise' sexuality at any point: in Dhasal's hands, it becomes starkly related to 'power' and 'domination' in the area of intimate human experiences.

Dilip Chitre[23] defines Dalit identity as that of a person uprooted several times in a single lifetime, a 'quintessentially lumpen, the constantly *degraded* human being.' Thus, the Dalit and the lumpen became Namdeo's central preoccupation as a creative writer, a political thinker and an activist. In an interview in 1982, he said that if the aim of social struggles was the removal of unhappiness, then poetry was necessary because it expressed that happiness vividly and powerfully. Later he stated, "Poetry is politics". Dhasal adheres to this principle in his private life. He told the photographer Henning Stegmüller, "I enjoy discovering myself. I am happy when I am writing a poem, and I am happy when I am leading a protest of prostitutes fighting for their rights."

Dhasal was an immigrant to the industrial city of Mumbai from a remote village in Poona. Gail Omvedt[24] explains how Dhasal's poems depict the consciousness born out of a classic industrialised world juxtaposed with the miseries of village immigrants whose ignorance was symbolised by the illiterate, ignorant 'mother' who fails to perceive the enormous changes taking place in the world around and outside her. The 'mother' in Dhasal's hands becomes an almost dumb, mimetic figure rooted in mute submission to her 'fate'. In a poem titled "So that my Mother may be convinced"[25], Dhasal describes how caste society and male dominance deformed his mother making her a:

"machinery for the production of worms..."

In addition, the 'mother' being

"sucked dry all your life."

He leads on to reveal the ignorance of the 'mother',

"You didn't even moo once from the depths,
You didn't stir the sky with a shrill cry.
The earth didn't crack.
How easily you lived, wrapped in rhinoceros hide."

He says this with a tinge of complexity and anger both at his mother's silence as well as long internalised Dalit resignation to oppression. He explores the borders of impossibility built around the idea of Dalit existence, which cannot be breached. This is to say that concepts such as easy life, happiness, freedom to choose et cetera flourish outside this border but have no tangible meaning inside it. In the poem, he goes on to suggest that for Dalits who have been denied everything material, their sole valuable possession could only be language itself and its subversive potential. Its potential power could be employed to name oppression and detail the forms of its existence thereby becoming a form of insurgency against subjugation. This belief in a dissident language's liberating character is echoed in the poem where he begs his mother not to "forecast defeat for the weapon" that is, language and poetry- "that the twentieth century has put into your son's hands" and which if used correctly will become the voice of all who "have lost their identity".

In the poem "Man, you should explode"[26], he charts out a "song of man" very much on the lines of legendary American poet Walt Whitman's "The Song of Myself". Dhasal uses a stinging and violent imagery similar to that of Whitman.

"Man, you should explode
Yourself to bits to start with..."

"You should be ready to carve out anybody's innards
without batting an eyelid

Commit murders and kill the sleeping ones..."

He sheds light on the commonplace reality of the kind of life people in the ghettos of Golpitha are forced to lead. He says,

"Cut the throat of your own kith and kin by conning
them; poison them, jinx them

You should hump anyone's mother or sister anywhere
you can..."

He goes on to trample religion, which plays no meaningful role in the life of the unprivileged, and the marginalised saying,

"One should hang to death the descendents of Jesus,
the Paighambar, the Buddha and Vishnu

One should crumple up temples, churches, mosques,
sculptures, museum

One should blow with cannonballs all priests

And inscribe epigraphs with cloth soaked in their
blood"

Dhasal continues in a surrealist vein,

"...one should plan to die groaning and screaming in
pain

Let all this grow into tumor to fill the universe, balloon
up

And burst at a nameless time to shrink..."

And finally spells out his vision of a casteless egalitarian existence

"After this, all those who survive should...

...stop calling one another names–white or black,
Brahmin, *kshatriya*, *vaishya* or *shudra*...

> One should regard the sky as one's grandpa, the earth as one's grandma
>
> And coddled by them everybody should bask in mutual love…"

This is precisely the reason why Dhasal's translator Dilip Chitre[27] calls him a 'great poet'. Chitre believes that Dhasal understands that great poetry '*integrates*' rather than '*divides*' humanity.

In another poem, "Mandakini Patil: A young prostitute, My intended collage"[28] he uses the female prostitute of Golpitha, an object of carnal 'love' but still 'loathed'. She has no institutionalised sanctity like a wife and her dignity as a human being is denied and negated. For Dhasal, she is the ultimate *untouchable*, serving other humans by degrading oneself. The poem conjures a violent landscape

> "On a barren blue canvas
>
> clothes ripped off, a thigh blasted open
>
> A sixteen year old girl surrendering herself to pain
>
> And a pig: its snout full of blood"

The young prostitute here is a symbol of *double marginalisation*. Prostitutes are generally seen as nameless commodities for mere carnal pleasure of the dominant sex. Dhasal subverts this by not only *naming* the prostitute-'Mandakini', but also granting her a *surname* –'Patil'. At the same time, he is highlighting the violence against the prostitutes, which always goes unnoticed. Even lawfully wedded wives are not spared. Dhasal says,

> "Wives are the licensed whores of men.
>
> Men are the pimps and lovers of their wives."

He is taking on the role of bestowing voice to the voiceless as he invokes multiple subjectivities – the exploited prostitute, the betrayed lover, the enraged individual as well as at times, an unseeming *flaneur*-like detached figure. He describes what he has been witness to, since his very childhood, a merciless reality in the red light district of Mumbai. The casualness of expression that is evident here springs from both an experiential aesthetics as well as a kind of valorisation of bare existence. It foregrounds a new kind of realism and a new sense of 'beauty' challenging the idea of 'the sublime and the beautiful'. Another contemporary Dalit literary spearhead Sharankumar Limbale[29] has worked on similar concerns in a seminal work in the field entitled "*Towards an Aesthetic of Dalit Literature*".

> In his poem "Song of the republic and the dog"[30], he reports that the Dalit inhabits
>
> "the dark empire of hunger,
>
> The guts which have run dry…"

The Dalit empire is a place of chronic malnourishment, both physical as well as epistemological deprivation peopled by slum dwellers, leather workers, labourers, Prostitutes and so on. The Dalit life is mirrored by only one another creature–the leashed dog that:

> "howls and barks from time to time.
>
> This is his constitutional right.
>
> He lives on stale crumbs.
>
> His mind is calloused with endured injustice.
>
> If at a rebellious moment it becomes unbearable,
>
> And he jerks at his leash, tries to break his chain,
>
> Then he is shot."

The systematic and continuous silencing of any rebellion from below is highlighted here.

Another poem, "*Kamatipura*"[31] is even more startling in its unusual and stark representation of the peripheral,

> "The nocturnal porcupine reclines here
>
> Like an alluring grey bouquet

Wearing the syphilitic sores of centuries..."

These lines hardly need elucidation given the lucid and uninhibited acknowledgement of the Dalit existence in *Kamatipura*. The image of the thorny porcupine, coupled with that of a paradoxically 'alluring' (?) grey bouquet and the deadly venereal disease mingles quite effortlessly to foreground a clear-eyed view of Mumbai's oldest red-light area of *Kamatipura*. Here, Dhasal continues,

"Man has lost his speech

His God is a shitting skeleton..."

indicating perhaps, the meaninglessness of religion and an absolute loss of human expression. He speaks plainly, juxtaposing life with anti-life like hell, saying,

"This is hell.

This is a swirling vortex

This is an ugly agony

Death gathers here, as do words."

Dhasal is lamenting and at the same time, exhorting *Kamatipura* to let the 'lotus' bloom in its dirty waters perhaps as a symbol of hope and optimism, validating his commitment to its soil.

"Tucking all seasons under your armpit,

You squat in the mud here

I go beyond all the pleasures and pains of whoring and wait

For your lotus to bloom,

-A lotus in the mud."

Dilip Chitre[32] visualises these very slums of *Kamatipura* surviving like '... lesions, sores, festering wounds, or malignant tumors hidden in Mumbai's 'superficially glamorous anatomy'.

Moving on to the reception history of Dhasal's poetry, interestingly, Dhasal was awarded the Maharashtra State Award in 1973 and the Nehru Award in 1974 for *Golpitha*. This could indicate, in my view, an attempt on the part of the state to appropriate the dissident voice into the mainstream in a deeper silencing of the marginalised. It could also be seen as an attempt by the authority to channelise the revolt, the acidic torrent of anger of the suppressed by embellishing it with awards and recognition. Dhasal[33] himself vehemently claims, "Until now, I remain an activist with a deep awareness of the problem of untouchability and its far reaching consequences." He explains his revolt against the mainstream politics and the canonical literature "I boozed. I visited brothels… It was life! Then, I threw all rulebooks out. No longer the rules of prosody for me. My poetry was as free as I was. I had found my weapons and I sharpened them." American scholar Dr Eleanor Zelliot[34] has stated that the "most important poet in Dalit literature in recent times is Namdeo Dhasal, as no one can beat Dhasal in the powerful imagery, evocative language and bold statements against the system". It would be fitting to conclude this broad analysis of Dhasal's poetry with Romila Thapar's statement[35] "Traditions are not self created: they are consciously chosen ..." As Dhasal's poetry continues to inspire and startle many to stand up, take notice as well as carry forward the torch of protest that he has defiantly ignited.

CONCLUSION

In the first part of the paper, I tried to provide an overview of the emergence of the category of Dalit literature as shaped by Phule and Ambedkar. I talked about the two major phases of Dalit writing – the first led by the likes of Baburao Bagul etc., with emphasis on the second and better recognised revival of Dalit writing with Namdeo Dhasal leading the charge. In the second section of the paper, I looked at the major biographical details of the person Namdeo and the important events in his life. In the final section by studying some of his poems, I tried to examine how Dhasal's exercise of mapping the "self" is inextricably intertwined with the process of mapping dalithood. Admittedly, his turnover from the '*messiah*' of Dalits to Right wing Politics in the later stage of his literary career remains unexplored and could definitely be subjected to a wider examination and evaluation on a different platform.

Notes

1 Dangle, Arjun - 1992, "*The Poisoned Bread*"; Orient Longman, Bombay.

2. Apte, V.S. - 1998, *Sanskrit Dictionary*, Motilal Banarasidas Pvt. Ltd.

3. Bhagat, Datta – 1992, "*Dalit Sahitya: Disha ani Dishantar*"; Abhay prakashan.

4. Dangle, Arjun - 1992, "*The Poisoned Bread*" – introduction to; Orient Longman, Bombay.

5. Ambedkar, B.R. – 1945, '*Gandhism: The Doom of Untouchables*' in "What Gandhi and Congress Have Done to the Untouchables"; Thacker, Bombay.

6. Dirks, Nicholas B. – 2002, "*Castes of Mind- Colonialism and the Making of Modern India*"; Permanent Black.

7. Deo, Veena - 1996, Chapter 13 -'*Dalit Literature in Marathi*' in "Handbook of Twentieth Century Literatures in India"; Ed. by-Nalini Natarajan, Greenwood Press.

8. *Ibid*.

9. Punalekar, S.P. -2001, '*Dalit Literature and Dalit Identity*' in "Dalit identity and Politics"; Sage Publications.

10. Dangle, Arjun - 1992, "*The Poisoned Bread*" – introduction to; Orient Longman, Bombay.

11. Chitre, Dilip – 2007, '*Poetry of the Scum of the Earth*' in "Namdeo Dhasal: Poet of the Underworld, Poems 1972-2006"; Narayana Publishing.

12. Chitre, Dilip – 2007, '*Namdeo's Mumbai*' in "Namdeo Dhasal: Poet of the Underworld, Poems 1972-2006"; Narayana Publishing.

13. Kumar, Raj – 2010, *Dalit Personal Narratives: Reading Caste, Nation and Identity*; Orient BlackSwan. p. 146.

14. Rajawat, Mamta – 2004, "*Encyclopaedia of Dalits in India*", Vol. 1, History of Dalits; Anmol Publications; New Delhi.

15. Kulkarni, G.M. and Pundalik, Vidyadhar – 1992, "*Dalit Literature: a Sociocultural Study*"; Sugava Prakashan, Pune.

16. Deshpande, Sudhanva – 2007, "*Superstar Dhasal*" in Frontline Magazine, July 2007.

17. Satchidanandan, K. -1999, '*Imagined Communities: Collective aspirations in Contemporary Indian Poetry*', in "Many Indias, Many Literatures – New Critical Essays"; Ed. by Shormishtha Panja, Worldview Publications.

18. Basu, Tapan -2002, '*Narratives of Suffering: Dalit Perspectives*' in "Translating Caste" Ed. by – Tapan Basu; Katha Publications.

19. Punalekar, S.P. -2001, '*Dalit Literature and Dalit Identity*' in "Dalit identity and Politics"; Sage Publications.

20. Dhasal, Namdeo - 2007, '*Namdeo on Namdeo*' in "Namdeo Dhasal: Poet of the Underworld, Poems 1972-2006" ed. by- Dilip Chitre; Narayana Publishing.

21. Jaaware, Aniket – 1998, '*Eating, and Eating with, the Dalit: a Re-consideration Touching upon Marathi Poetry*' in "Indian Poetry; Modernism and After" (A Seminar), 2001, ed. by – K. Satchidanandan; Sahitya Akademi.

22. Deo, Veena - 1996, Chapter 13 -'*Dalit Literature in Marathi*' in "Handbook of Twentieth Century Literatures in India"; Ed. by-Nalini Natarajan; Greenwood Press.

23. Chitre, Dilip – 2007, '*Namdeo's Mumbai*' in "Namdeo Dhasal: Poet of the Underworld, Poems 1972-2006"; Narayana Publishing.

24. Omvedt, Gail – 2006, '*Hinduism as Feudal backwardness: The Dalit Panthers*' in "Dalit Visions"; Orient Longman.

25. I have used Dilip Chitre's Translation (2007) of Dhasal's poems in his book- "Namdeo Dhasal: Poet of the Underworld, Poems 1972-2006"; Narayana Publishing.

26. Ibid.

27. Chitre, Dilip – 2007, '*Poetry of the Scum of the Earth*' in "Namdeo Dhasal: Poet of the Underworld, Poems 1972-2006"; Narayana Publishing.

28. Dilip Chitre's Translation (2007) of Dhasal's poems in his book- "Namdeo Dhasal: Poet of the Underworld, Poems 1972-2006"; Narayana Publishing.

29. Limbale, Sharankumar – 2004, "Towards an Aesthetic of Dalit Literature", Orient Longman, Delhi: 2004. Also, one can look up Omprakash Valmiki's "*Dalit Sahitya ka Saundarya Shastra*" (2001) a critical work on the aesthetics of Dalit Literature, and his crucial autobiography '*Joothan: A Dalit's Life'*, tr. from Hindi by Arun Prabha Mukherjee; Samya Prakashan, Kolkata: 2003.

30. Dilip Chitre's Translation (2007) of Dhasal's poems in his book- "Na*mdeo Dhasal*:" Poet of the Underworld, Poems 1972-2006"; Narayana Publishing.

31. *Ibid*.

32. Chitre, Dilip – 2007, '*Namdeo's Mumbai*' in "Namdeo Dhasal: Poet of the Underworld, Poems 1972-2006"; Narayana Publishing.

33. Dhasal, Namdeo - 2007, '*Namdeo on Namdeo*' in "Namdeo Dhasal: Poet of the Underworld, Poems 1972-2006" ed. by- Dilip Chitre; Narayana Publishing.

34. Zelliot, Eleanor – 1992, "*An Anthology of Dalit Literature*"; Gyan Publishing House, New Delhi.

35. Thapar, Romila – 1987, '*Tradition*' in "Cultural Transaction in Early India- Tradition and Patronage"; OUP.

11

Reading Resistance in Dalit Women's Autobiographies

Putul Sathe

The arrival of dalit literary criticism and dalit literature located within the Ambedkarite movement was accompanied by a new founded dalit political identity and social consciousness. In this context G.N. Devy has identified dalit writings as one of the forces, which have challenged the bourgeois nationalist perspective in Indian literary historiography. Within dalit literature, autobiography is a literary and cultural expression of internal caste based discrimination. As cultural and literary expression dalit autobiographies have created a praxis, which has challenged existing literary structures through their articulation of cultural and caste based discrimination:

The literary historiography of dalit literature[is derived] from this principle of racial inequality of Indian society. It focuses on the question of otherness, difference, marginality, canon and the categories of aesthetics. In order to voice the protest of the marginalised, dalit literature often follows the subversive historiographic path of personalising history. It is therefore, . . ., that autobiography is the most potent and often exercised form of fiction produced in dalit literature. (Devy, 2009 : 129)

Dalit autobiographies governed by "subversive historiographic path of personalising history" becomes a political gesture in the context of Indian literary historiography to focus upon a sort of "epistemic mutations" (Mohanty, 1998:120) not only in "cultural criticism but in social and historiography as well" (120). The agenda of personalising history point to the central political claim of the autobiographical narratives that certain subaltern sensitivities have been repressed or left unarticulated. As cultural narratives, the autobiographies emerge as site of articulation of resistance creating the possibility for representation of the self and the community. The present paper will focus on Urmila Pawar's *The Weave of My Life* (2008) and Baby Kamble's *The Prisons We Broke* (2008) as narratives of resistance, which project voices of previously silenced subaltern women to create emancipatory spaces. As narratives of resistance they are small voices located on the margin of social and cultural imagination traversing the realm of dalit literature and women's autobiographical writings.

Sharankumar Limbale in his book Towards an Aesthetics of Dalit Literature: History, Controversies and Considerations (2004) had drawn to the rise of alternative literary paradigms by dalit writers through their resistance to caste based discrimination in their writings. Hence, dalit literary and cultural representations have moved beyond the 'discourse of pity', which was the case in the works of upper caste writers. The articulation of resistance was wedded to identity politics and Arjun Dangle has advocated the 'differentness' to understand this different literary–ideological-cultural paradigm.

Within the field of autobiographical writing, women's autobiographies emerge as site of difference, since they provided an alternative to 'maleness' of autobiographies written by men and simultaneously within the category 'woman'. As a polyphonous sign in a double voiced discourse, autobiographies by women are performances which have negotiated with a seamless, decentred self. Autobiographical writings have been "one of the most important sites of feminist debate precisely because it demonstrates that there are many different ways of writing the subject" (Anderson, 2007: 87). In the context of women's writing in India, women could write about only a few things in the absence of a sustained, high level of formal education. Beginning in the 19th century, it was high caste Hindu women, who started writing autobiographies which were located in the new emerging material and social condition resulting from reforms and legislative innovation in public sphere. Hence, the autobiographies revolved around *sati*, widow remarriage, child marriage, divorce and the age of consent (Sarkar, 1999). Women's autobiographies then became site, where tension were articulated resulting from colonial modernity. The dominant ideology of nineteenth century cultural nationalism celebrated India's spirituality superiority over material West and remained silent about caste/gender based humiliation and was not concerned about racial humiliation. The autobiographies of upper caste women have to be located within this framework. The question of caste was invisible in their writings. Sharmile Rege in her study of autobiographies in Marathi written by upper caste women has drawn attention to this erasure:

> . . . the majority of modern Brahmin women's autobiographies have been narratives of upper caste women, their struggles with tradition and their desire to be modern. It is this self that claims to be universal, modern unmarked by caste through its journeys of companionate marriage, modern institutions and marital discord. Caste is the 'other' of the modern as if it belongs only to Dalit women. This claim of the upper caste women's autobiography to represent modern Marathi/Indian women serves, on the other hand, to render invisible their complicity in privileges of brahminical patriarchy; and on the other, it classifies the narratives of women whose self-definition is located explicitly in caste as a relational identity, as if it were the 'other' of modern and feminist. (Rege, 2006: 50)

Within this paradigm dalit women's autobiographies through their articulation of caste based inequalities traced the "hidden histories of hurt and humiliation" (Rao 2003: 3) and as gendered texts was an initiative to engage with dalit and social patriarchy. Writing of resistance brought to forefront gendered subaltern alternative historical voices of politicised activist dalit women and underscored the epistemological disadvantages of unmarked feminism (S. Anand, 2009). Dalit women's autobiographies through their struggles and literary representations have questioned the genealogy of Indian feminism where the position of caste has not been articulated and drew attention to the complex relationship between feminism and caste's complex history. Anupama Rao as probed the specificity of this position.

Dalit feminism poses anew the position of how we might understand caste's complex history as a form of identification and as a structure of disenfranchisement and exploitation, how we revisit the forgotten and repressed histories that illuminate the criticism of feminism by its most vulnerable and exploited constituency (Rao, 3).

Baby Kamble's text can be located within the existing oeuvre of protest writing in Marathi. According to Maya Pandit the translator of Baby Kamble's autobiography, this autobiography is probably the first autobiography by a dalit women in Marathi. Most of the dalit autobiogra phies written by men were for a mixed readership of dalit and non-dalit readers. This narrative on the other hand is not only a text representative of the dalit community but is an engagement with the "history of Dalit oppression"(Kamble, 2008: IX) and is "located in the tradition of direct self-assertion" (IX). The text confronts Brahminical hegemony and patriarchal structures within dalit society. Located on the margins of 'social imaginary', the representation of marginality writes resistance and the text is cultural site with "tremendous transformative potential for oppressed people" (XI). This performance is not an individual act but is collective in nature:

I wrote about what my community experienced. The suffering of my people became my own suffering. Their experiences became mine. So I really find it very difficult to think of myself outside of my community (136).

Articulation of collective experience is a political act of resistance and in the process the autobiography becomes a socio-biography and creates a subject position, which is at once individual and collective. The autobiographer is "simultaneously the author of an individuated act of truth-telling and the subject of a shared historical memory" (Udayakumar, 2008:421). The articulation of subjectivity violates the concept violated the concept of singular individual self and the narrative voice that "narrates the humiliation has questioned the hegemonic power of the dominant Brahminic authority" (Ramakrishnan, 2011:69). Articulation of humiliation becomes a mode of understanding the social system of 'graded inequality' embedded in the caste system from the point of view of a gendered untouchable identity. The experience of untouchability was both a "layered experience and . . . an evil that is stunning in its banality" (Geeta, 2009: 92). Addressing the hegemonic nature of caste structure the text registrars resistance and the narrative point to "moral corruption of the society which legitimises caste oppression. (Ramakrishnan, 67):

> Such was the condition of our people. We were just like animals, but without tails. We could be called human because we had two legs instead of four. Otherwise there was no difference between us and the animals. But how had we been reduced to this bestial state? Who was responsible? Who else, but people of the high caste! They destroyed our reasoning, our ability (Kamble, 49).

Articulation of resistance is articulation of marginality and is located within the 'discourse of participation', which is "framed in terms of sympathetic immediacy, performative speech acts and ritual action"(Pandhian, 2008:40). In keeping with this choice, the autobiography is not about centralising a single person and the text is distanced from the "formal and establish the ordinary as [the] chosen domain" (35). The text describes the childhood of Baby Kamble as part of community life, the struggles of dalit society, celebration of festivals, rituals performed at dalit weddings, the impact of Ambedkarite movement, the plight of dalit women and the world of dalit labouring body. The act of narrativising the "ordinary' raise moral issues that cannot be addressed in purely artistic or socio-political terms (Ramakrishnan, 2011) and the text creates a cultural space that brings out how "experience, affect and politics are inseparable" (Pandhian, 40).

The recounting of humiliation along the multiple axis of gender, class and caste is not a victim narrative, rather is a mode of resistance to the hegemony of caste system. Caste structure used structural violence to maintain caste hierarchy and this was "integral to the molecular structure of caste" (Rao, 2011:114). The labouring body of the *Mahar* women was the marker of caste and women's subordination was the gateway to caste system. Humiliation as Gopal Guru has pointed out is an individual, collective, social and political phenomenon. Dalit women's experience of caste based humiliation results in the visibility of caste, which scripts a polemical attack on gender and caste structures of brahminical patriarchy. Within this paradigm the dalit women is also located within dalit patriarchy and experiences the worst form of exploitation when dalit men do not hesitate in chopping off the nose of those dalit women who fail to conform to dalit patriarchal norms (Kamble 98). The body of the violated dalit women provide a critique of dalit patriarchy and destroys the myth of dalit patriarchy as democratic. Dalit women negotiate not with multiple patriarchies, but with what Uma Chakravarti has termed as 'graded patriarchies' operating within the grid of brahminical patriarchy.

Moving beyond literary paradigms, as part of protest literature the text has to be located and read within the larger counter discourse of Amdekarite movement, which questioned the liberal, unified humanist vision of a nation controlled by elites, who tried to "control and regulate the unchartered spaces of living communities" (Ramakrishnan 71). As a site of this articulation the text spells out the tenants of Ambedkarite project, which was not an abstract one but brought to the centre stage of Indian political modernity the stigmatised dalit community as a political community. The autobiography maps the journey of dalits, who were "history's losers" (Rao, 2011:208) to create a "crucial space of alterity" (208) not through "ameliorative logic of a reformed Hinduism" (209) but by existing from brahminical fold through conversion to Buddhism.

Urmila Pawar's autobiography titled 'The Weave of My Life'(2008) has been categorised as a "A Dalit Woman's Memoirs" and the metaphor of woven things runs throughout the narrative. Woven together the text is made up of several texts and inscribes a complex notion of the margin. The trajectory of Urmila Pawar is very different in terms of modern education, salaried employment and involvement in women's movement which takes her away from the world of physical labour and struggle for livelihood. Dalit autobiography as a literary and cultural genre as pointed out after 'The Prisons we Broke' were life narratives, which brought out struggles of *shudra* (low caste) and *atishudra* (Dalits) men and women but one perceives the emergence of individual identity, which was in contrast to one's community and represented success stories resulting from affirmative action of the state and the onset of neo-liberal programmes during the 1980s and 1990s. Narendra Jadhav's autobiography is representative of a life story of a de-caste dalit. But at the same time atrocities against dalits still continue. Pawar's autobiography traverses a range of positions, representing 'graded margininalities' and can be read as a "complex narrative of a gendered individual who looks at the world initially from her location within the caste but who also goes on to transcend the caste identity from a feminist perspective" (Pawar, 2008: XVII). Pawar's autobiography is both a continuation of the tradition of Baby Kamble of portraying the inhuman condition of the community, but it moves forward where caste identities morphed into a larger human identity influenced by Buddhist philosophy. The dialectics between self and community finds a larger articulation with Pawar re-defining the category 'Dalit' to include a radical humanist category:

'Dalit'! How are we Dalit now? They asked angrily. We had to make an elaborate explanation: Dalit does not mean socially oppressed people. It also signals rational, secular people who have discarded the oppressive system and concepts like God, fate and caste system.

Pawar's re-definition of Dalit as a radical liberating agency while promoting "grater historical sensitivity"(Pawar, 325) marks the arrival of a gendered self as "situated, local and partial" (329) along the multiple axis of class, caste and gender. Intersectionality as a particular perspective draws upon marginalised subjects inscribing the belief the ". . . those who have experienced discrimination speak with a special voice to which we should listen" (Matsuda quoted in Nash, 2008: 3).

The memoirs present a detailed account of the community along with Pawar's journey to emerge as a feminist, thereby the issue of 'difference' to the centre stage. The narrative opens with a detailed description of the labouring dalit women travelling from nearby villages to the market at Ratnagiri to sell various things through a hilly and dangerous terrain:

Women were compelled to make the journey to the market for they had to sell their wares for survival. (Pawar, 2).

The articulation of resistance occurs through mapping of hurt and humiliation across various structures and practices. The culture of backbreaking physical labour has been documented in great detail, when Pawar recalls the hardship of women, who went to collect oysters and crabs in the middle of the creek, bending down in knee deep water and returned with their hands bruised and bleeding. Some of them were drowned while bending in deep water and did not notice the water level rising. Enacting the violence embedded in caste identity draws attention to the lived reality of dalit women, which the text throughout will vividly portray.

At another level the writing of resistance is the moment, when the narrator wakes up to the implication of being a member of low caste (Ramakrishnan, 721). There are several such episodes in the text. One such episode is when Pawar goes to deliver the baskets to her mother customers and she would be made to stand outside their houses at the threshold. Pawar would then put the baskets down and the customers would "sprinkle water on them to wash away the pollution, and only then would touch them" (Pawar, 65) and would "drop coins in my hands from above, avoiding contact as if their hands would have burnt had they touched me" (65).

The act of writing of resistance is a performance in the public domain with certain ideological underpinnings, which call for a revision of the dichotomy between the self and the society, the private and the public and the question the legitimacy of narratives that inform the history of the nation. Dalit life narratives are 'testimonios', which forge the right to speak both for and beyond the individual and contest explicitly or implicitly the official forgetting of histories of caste operation, struggles and resistance (Rege, 13) and hence the narrative demands "new modes of narration and signification" (Ramakrishnan, 66).

Central to both the texts is the articulation of a Dalit feminist standpoint which results in the creation of cultural and literary space, which is concerned with the recovery of Dalit gendered discourse. This discourse has provided a critique of the failure of dominant groups to critically and systematically interrogate their advantaged situation in terms of knowledge production and leaves them crippled, scientifically and epistemologically (Rege, 328).

Within this literary space reading resistance calls for an engagement with marginalised gendered voices and involves understanding the "complex relationships of social location, experience and history" (Rege, 72) and results in building dalit feminist pedagogies. This site include a range of possible meanings and knowledge systems both from dominant and radical discourses. Re-visiting the margin and centre results in reading and understanding resistance that moves beyond "epistemic charity" (Rege, 73). And finally the category literature in this context included literature, history and politics and calls for a need to produce new and liberating revisions of history.

12

Dalit Voices and Problem of Communication

N.V. Sangvikar

Communication emerges out to be the most crucial problem in all spheres of life. There have been various studies on communication, notably in the field of linguistics, media and social sciences. In spite of the numerous studies on communication, it remains an enigma. Modern literature has intensified the problems of communication, by highlighting the failure of communication. The most noticeable post-war dramatic treatment of communication is to be found in the theatre of absurd, which completely inverts all norms of communication. The absurd playwrights like Beckelt, Ionesco, Genet and others state through their plays that communication is not possible among human beings, due to their emotional, social and philosophical alienation from one another. These plays present a semantic impasse through their dialogues, whereby the characters struggle to capture meanings.

Communication is a social process. Therefore, the role, status and position of individuals influence their communication. As a corollary to the above, it follows that by studying the pattern of communication among a given set of participants, it is possible to discover the underlying social structure. When individuals communicate with one another, they are conscious of their position in the social structure. As a result, in modern societies it is not possible to have innocent and direct communication among participants. Sometimes there are conflicts of roles among the participants in a given communicative event. In such a situation the meanings are not stable, which gives rise to various ambiguities of communication.

The actions in a social system are influenced by the nature of social organisation. For example, social relations may be of various types, depending on the social structure. If the structure is very rigid, the social relations are mediated by the power of individuals, which they hold by virtue of their being at particular nodes in the social hierarchy. Talcott Parsons has proposed a three-tier structure of social acts (Savage, 1981: 132), when they are concretised. This implies that any social act has to be viewed not in terms of one, but three systems. These three systems belong to the personality of individuals, social and cultural systems (Savage 1981). The personality aspect of a social act refers to the 'need-dispositions' of human beings. The social level incorporates the 'role-expectation', whereas the cultural domain includes the 'value-orientation'. Talcott Parson has thus revolutionised the sociological understanding of observable human behaviour.

Talcott Parsons' views on social system imply an emphasis on the relationship of social actors to one another (Savage 1981). The psychological and cultural factors seem to provide two extremes in understanding social acts. On the one hand, a psychological perspective entails a kind of reductionism; on the other hand, the cultural paradigm necessitates idealism. Therefore, a balanced approach to the understanding of social phenomena is to relate them to the social system with its particular structure. Stressing this observation, Savage (1981: 131) says:

The social system is a system of action in which actions are organised around the relations of actors to each other, i.e. interaction. The elementary conceptual unit of the social system is the 'role'. Roles involve individual personalities, but what distinguishes role action from merely individual action is the differentiation of the action elements involved. Interaction is governed by a distinct mode or organisation, by problems of a different functional character than those experienced by the personality system.

The implication of Parsons' concept of social system is that it makes it possible to study social structure in a relatively culture-free universal framework. This happens because what are to be studied are not so much the cultural features of a particular society, but the aspects of system. Parsons' views hint at the possibility of defining social structure as a category in a universal sense. Moreover, Parsons has emphasised the role of interaction in the manifestations of particular social acts. Therefore, by studying the nature of interaction among people, it is possible to discuss the social structure.

Having thus resolved the cultural intervention in the ordering of social life, it is now imperative to attend to the importance of communication in concretising social reality. Any interaction among individuals can be studied only by observing the pattern of interpersonal communication. This is because it is through communication that the individuals express their attitudes to one another. The power that mediates human relationships can be studied through communication. It is a matter of common understanding that modern individuals have multiple social identities, due to the complex network of social structure which defines their identity. Thus, theoretically speaking, there cannot be a consistent pattern of communication specific to a particular individual. This is because of the changes in his/her social role across the social structure. These various roles may often contradict one another and place the individual in a situation of predicament. The problems of communication in a given situation are neither psychological nor linguistic. In fact, the problems of communication are the indicators of the pressures of social structure on individuals. Since the researcher has chosen to think of social structure in terms of Parsons' abstract notion of social system, it is possible to study the problem of communication with reference to social structure, without fearing any distortion of analysis due to non-familiarity with specific cultural aspects.

Communication can be studied from many perspectives. It has been studied within such separate disciplines as linguistics, philosophy, psychology and sociology. The basic situation in communication involves sending a message by an addresser to an addressing, using a code shared by both. Thus, sharedness in communication is the first pre-requisite for successful communication. It is this shraedness that makes communication a social process. There are broadly speaking, two kinds of study on communication, micro-level and macro-level. In a micro-level study, the emphasis is on the features employed in dialogues between individuals. Within the field of linguistics, a number of approaches are available to study communication from this perspective. This approach of studying interpersonal communication has generated several models within the broad sub-field of discourse analysis. Similarly, a sociolinguistic study of communication has been greatly facilitated by insights within pragmatics, particularly the speech Act Theory and the Co-operative Principle of H.P. Grice.

Psychoanalysis, whose originator is Sigmund Freud, has influenced several disciplines within Humanities. The studies of communication too have been influenced by various psychological insights, notably psychoanalysis. Communication in literary texts within the psychoanalytic paradigm can be seen as a manifestation of the state of mind of characters. For example, Hamlet's soliloquies have been studied as a mode of communication that is characteristic of the working of human mind. Besides, within neurolinguistics, research has been going on to establish a correlation between language use and the human neurological system. Closely linked to the psychological approach to the study of communication is the philosophical perspective, which relates issues like morality and ethics to be process of communication.

It can be argued here that while the study of communication within linguistics, philosophy and psychology has relied on the micro-level manifestations, a sociological understanding of the process of communication necessitates a macro-level approach, because the range of sociological issues is wider than other disciplines within Humanities. Moreover, sociological studies have isolated various aspects of social structure, such as role, status, religion, nation, class and so on. Therefore, to arrive at a sociological theory of communication that would be able to take into account all the parameters of social structure, is indeed an idealistic proposition. The article has avoided different theoretical views on communication and social structure. Instead, he has taken the most basic meaning of the terms. The reason behind this decision is that the purpose of this study is not to indulge in a debate on the subtle definitions of communication and social structure, but to relate the two with each other.

As against the micro-level theories of communication, which can be traced back in history to Aristotle's rhetoric, the researcher has hypothesised in this study that communication among individuals in a given context reflects the social structure to which the individuals belong. This happens because the patterns of communication that become stabilised over a period of time are in fact, nothing but manifestations of social organisation. For example, greetings, politeness strategies, requests and other taken-for-granted aspects of everyday discourse depend on whether the society promotes hierarchies in social relations or equality of individuals. This is also the reason behind the variation of ritualistic or formulaic constructions from one culture to another.

Communication plays an important role in giving shape to social structure. All knowledge is basically a mode of communication. One of the ways of marginalising social groups is to exclude than form the process of communication. In George Orwell's famous novel 'Nineteen Eighty Four', the state exercises power over the citizens by using communication. Not only does communication have influence on the nature of individual relationships, but also the overall pattern of social relations in a society. As has been hinted earlier, the process of communication is socially significant. The mass media can alter the social reality by manipulating facts and presenting them in a manner that controls the lives of individuals. Social structure generates a hierarchical channel of communication, whether in private relationships or public spheres. For example, the effects of a rigid society are reflected in unusually hierarchical relationships within family. As a result, the members of such a family are unable to interact with each other in a natural manner.

The social effects of communication are widespread, some of which may be beyond the scope of this article. Communication operates in complex societies as a process of concretising the organisational structure. In order to insulate themselves from other groups, some social groups evolve highly specialised codes for communication. The bureaucracy, for example, controls human lives by evolving a code of communication which is different from that used by social actors in everyday life. Thus, communication is not a neutral process of exchanging information. It empowers social actors and gives rise to social organisation. On the model of public communication, individuals may also develop their private codes. The mannerisms and themes of communication of a group insulate it from other individuals.

In India, there has been a caste-based oppression of individuals. The so-called Dalits have, in fact, been marginalised by alienating them from all channels of public communication. In ancient times, the holy scriptures written in Sanskrit were not supposed to be read by the low caste people. In the contemporary society, the voice of Dalits is not allowed to reach the masses, by excluding them from mass media, since these are controlled by the upper castes. Of late, the rise of the tradition of Dalit literature can be seen as a protest at the level of communication. By representing and circulating images of the suffering of Dalits, the Dalits writers generating a debate in the society, which hopefully will empower the Dalits. The use of English as the medium of communication presents another case of communication being a tool of marginalisation. The use of English has created a class divide in the Indian society, leading to a double oppression of the Dalits. The English speaking Indians consider themselves superior to those who cannot speak or write English. This has altered the structure of Indian society.

The above discussion points to the fact that communication is closely related to various aspects of social structure. It manifests itself as a social process at least at three levels – form, theme and code. At the level of form, there are a number of inter-dependent manifestations of communication that are directly related to the social structure. For example, the forms of private communication, bureaucratic communication and ritualistic communication on social occasions are different from each other. Similarly, corresponding to the formal differences, the themes of communication vary according to its context. In multi-lingual societies like India, the presence of several languages generates the problem of communication at the level of code. The significance of the above discussion lies in the fact that it problematises the study of communication. Micro-level approaches to the study of dialogues, such as within discourse analysis and pragmatics, can at best reveal a limited perspective on communication. Therefore, the researcher has not followed any particular theory of communication. On the contrary, he has allowed the analysis to draw conclusions from all the three facts of communication, that is, form, theme and code, simultaneously.

Select References

1. Baker, James R. et. al (eds) (1970). *Twentieth Century Literature* Vol. 16: No. 1.
2. Barratt, William (1964). *What is Existentialism?* New York: Grove.
3. Bennett, Robert B. (1987). "*Tragic Vision in The Zoo Story*" in Parker, Dorothy (ed.) (1987). Essays on Modern American Drama: Williams, Miller, Albee and Shepard. Toronto: University of Toronto Press.
4. Braem, Helmut M. (1968). Edward Albee. Hannover: Velber Verlag.
5. Brustein, Robert (1964) The Theatre of Revolt: An Approach to Modern Drama. Boston: Little, Brown and Co.
6. Freedman, Morris (1971). American Drama in Social Context. Carbondale: Southern Illinois University Press.

7. Ravindran, R.K. (ed) (1999). *Hand book of Mass Communication*. New Delhi: Amol.
8. Savage Stephen P. (1981). *The Theories of Talcott Parsons: The Social Relations of Action*, New York: St. Martin's Press.
9. Zelliot, Eleanor (1992). *From Untouchable to Dalit: Essays on the Ambedkar Movement*. New Delhi: Manohar.

13

Dalit Representation and Reality: A Literary Perspective

Parmod Kumar

Introduction

The Caste System

Caste system has been the main instrument of exploitation since ages in the Indian society. The early class system in India had emerged as the varna system. The vast Hindus valley civilisation (2500-1800 BC) bore no signs of varna system, though it had class-division in embryonic form. The Aryans who entered Indian subcontinent from Central Asia (1200-1000BC) had three main sections within them – the Priests, Rajanyas, and dasyas – but this division was based on the duties they performed in their society rather than based on varna system. The local clans' people who were defeated over the conflicts for resources also generally termed as 'dasyas'.

The tribes that were defeated in the fight for water resources, and other resources from among Aryans and non-Aryans were treated as 'slaves'. These are called slaves during this period when the society was changing from pastoral – animal-rearing stage to the stage of development of food production. During Rig Vedic period the common people were termed as 'Vis' when the society was mainly pastoral. Later by 1000 BC by *Jajur* Vedic period these people were still called 'Vis' but denoted as agrarian communities. The Aryans had a collective ownership system over land, animals and other resources. The section of people who were referred as 'dasyas' became the collective lot who served the Aryans and non Aryans – who were mainly victorious in the conflicts.

Varna System

Gradually, the clan system based on blood relations was collapsed while the 'Rajanya' (priestly) section divided into Kshatriyas and Brahmins. These two categories of people lived on the gifts presented to them by the defeated sections. 'Vis' section turned into 'Vysya' having agriculture as the main occupation. Eventually all the subordinated sections both 'Aryans' and 'non-aryans' – who were called 'dasyas' came to be known as '*sudras*'. But all sudras were not 'slaves'. Some took the job of animal-rearing while other participated in agricultural production. Thus, 'varna' system emerged from the clan system as the agricultural production becomes the main mode of social development. Thus, varna system started emerging around 1000 BC and was stabilised by 600 BC. In India, varna system was emerged from early Adivasi social groupings instead of 'slave system' that was the main characteristic of European societal development due to the interaction and conflicts that occurred between the local inhabitants and 'Aryans' who were clashed and collided as they belonged to different stages of development.

The vast Indian sites of habitation and settlement with large resources for food gathering and hunting, Roman type of slave system was unlikely to develop in India. Aryans who were in advanced stage of development compare to the local communities when they arrived in the sub-continent played decisive role in what was to come later along with the advanced section of the local communities.

Aryan and Non-Aryan Division

Popular perception traces it to the Aryan invansion of India and links it to the process by which the invaders subjugated the indig-enous inhabitants. Thus, it is believed that the castes — Brahmans, Kshatriyas and Vaishyas — have descended primarily from the original Aryans or invaders from outside, while the masses of Sudras, untouchables and tribal people — the vast majority of the Indian people — have descended from the conquered non-Aryan indigenous people. However, this as an inadequate explanation of caste, as it does not explain how the invasion, in itself, could create the complex struc-tures of caste, and how caste seems stron-gest in areas least affected by these invasions. Also there is no historical evidence of such a massive and sudden invasion of outsiders in the period concerned-2090 to 1000 BC. In fact the 'invasions' took the form of successive waves over a long period of time. The Aryans and later invaders adjusted and modified this system and provided it with a firm ideological foundation.

Whatever may be the case, it is clear that from earliest times that caste functioned as the specific form, in which unpaid surplus labour is pumped out of the direct producers. Through the caste system, class was "fixed"' by birth in a particular caste which has a particular status within a broad hierarchy of castes. The rigidity of the system is maintained by strict rules of acceptable occupation or range of occupations, marriages within caste, taboos against inter-dining and maintaining close social relations outside caste *(roti-beti-vyavhar)*.

The Ideological Base of the Caste System

The maintenance of the caste system formed an integral part of the value system formulated at that time, both at the philosophical level and in terms of social conduct. Thus, the *Purushasukta* (one of the later hymns of the *Rig Veda*) created the mythology of the four castes representing the various parts of the primeval being; and their status being determined by the parts they represent —*Brahmans* the mouth, *Kshatriyas* the arms, Vaishyas the thighs and Sudras the feet. The ritual status of each caste depends on the supposed 'purity' of each caste. This 'purity' was maintained by distance from labour. Thus, the Brahmans took over the highest sta-tus as the most pure caste by refusing to do any form of labour. Their exclusive sphere was that of "knowledge". Sudras rendered, "impure" by performing labour were condemned to low, exploited status and any incursion into the brahmanical sphere of knowledge, even inadvertently, was to be punished. The *dharmasastras* recommended pouring molten metal into the ears of Sudras who even accidentally heard the scriptures. The *Dharmasastras* and especially the codes of the *Manusnriti* prescribe the most vicious punishment for such and other violations of the caste taboos, against the Sudras.

The Untouchables and Women in the Caste System

A large mass of people were kept outside the pale of the caste system, even though they were an integral part of society—the untouchables. Denied any right of possession of land and other property they were condemned to a sub-human existence—even their shadow was considered to be polluting. Women also were oppressed and accorded inhuman treatment, in the value system and actual Practice of Brahmanical Hinduism; though lower caste women enjoyed greater degree of freedom within their caste as opposed to upper caste women. Behind this however was the patriarchal notion of protecting the purity of the caste by severely restricting the freedom of women. The involvement of lower caste women in the production process also provided the basis for their relative freedom. This value system still pervades the entire being of Brahmanical Hinduism even though challenges to it arose repeatedly in history. Buddhism and Jainism in the 6th century BC, Virsaivism in the South in the 10th century AD and the Bhakti movement in the 12th to 14th century AD, did arise as strong and popular challenges to Brahmanical Hinduism but they failed to effect a transformation of society and in some cases got subsumed into Brahmanical Hinduism. Through the ages the Brahmans consolidated their power, made taboos more oppressive and stricter and increased the spread of the caste system to such an extent, that apart from a few places, such as the North East and small pockets of dense tribal population, no part of India is untouched by the caste system and Brahman oppression.

The caste system has survived through all socio-historical changes, through different modes of production and still exists as a pervasive presence, today. It is obvious that, along with this continuity the nature of the dynamic of the caste system also needs to be understood.

Caste System in Ancient and Medieval Periods

The modes of production that existed, at times simultaneously, in various parts of India also shaped the caste system. Thus in ancient times the main relations of exploitation were between the monarchical state with its upper caste officials and the majority of land owning peasantry which in turn exploited the lower caste artisans and semi-slave untouchable labourers. Under feudalism intermediaries were either appointed by the state or arose from amongst dominant peasant castes. The relation of production continued to be defined by the caste system. Thus access to produce within the village was almost never on the basis of market exchange, rather on harvest divisions made through caste—the services performed by each caste and the share traditionally claimed for such services (the *jajmani* system).

The Muslim rulers in no significant way altered this system; at times merely placing entire regions under their nobles as part of their *jagir or mansab,* preferring to leave untouched the relations of exploitation at the village level. In fact caste to a major degree penetrated the social milieu of Indian Muslims. As opposed to European feudalism where there were no birth limits to performance of specific occupations and impoverished families that lost their land could be forced to work as wage labour, the caste system gave a rigidity and permanence to class divisions which is peculiar to Indian feudalism. Nevertheless, it was from this system that mercantile capitalism had begun to develop in the later Mughal period.

Under British Colonial Rule

The organic growth of the Indian economy and society was however arrested by the imposition of British colonial rule. The British imperialists subordinated the entire Indian social and economic formations to the needs of development of capitalism in Britain. Emergent indigenous industry was destroyed and existing trade networks were taken over to facilitate naked colonial plunder. The application of "capitalist" concepts of land ownership subordinate to ever increasing British demands for revenue, caused the pauperisation of the country-side—a process often run simultaneously with commercialisation of agriculture and setting up of plantations. This form of 'capitalism', which disrupted the agrarian class structure without really challenging the power of the feudals, also brought a new consolidation of caste. Though at one level British policies weakened the pre-existing caste-defined access of land, the newly emerging semi-feudal landlords continued caste based exploitation in the villages. Further because of the subordination of the Indian economy to British imperialist interests the opening of new factories, mines and schools were limited and despite formal 'openness' the old upper caste elites had an overwhelming advantage in taking up the higher positions in the new economic and administrative structures.

The eagerness of the upper caste elites to take up these positions is marked by the ease with which English replaced the ancient Sanskrit and the medieval Persian as the language of the elite. The lower castes were recruited into the lower rungs as miners and unskilled labour and quickly forsaken as soon as the need for skilled labour grew. Thus, the establishment of the neo-feudal colonial economy on the whole maintained the gap between the traditional elites and the exploited, though it also opened up new opportunities to limited sections.

Through active political intervention the colonial masters also reconsolidated socially divisive identities of religion and caste to better manage this populous country. While the upper castes were best suited and most willing to act as their subordinates, within them interest groups and pressure groups also emerged which later grabbed the leadership of the anti-colonial movement. The British also used non-Brahman caste associations against these elements, as part of their divide and rule strategy.

In pursuance of the policy of divide and, rule the British also decided to use the census investigations to obtain and record the exact rank of each caste on the basis of "social precedence as recognised by native public opinion". In a context when an individual's rise in status is dependent on the stall is of his caste, this led to the phenomenon of the dominant castes vying with each other to, claim higher status. British policies, thus, played an important role in shaping the, caste system we know today.

Caste Movements and Upward Mobility in Some Sudras Castes

During the entire period of, British colonial rule a variety of factors contributed to the expansion of opportunities for the self-enhancement of castes. But apart from the caste associations of already dominant castes, which became pressure groups seeking favours of the British Raj, various backward caste movements also sprang up. In general two trends could be seen in these caste movements. In one trend the aim of upward mobility of the caste predominated. In this trend British loyalist attitudes also developed and they became politically divisive. The second trend was more radical, it spread in villages, using the vernacular rather than English and attacking the entire caste system rather than claiming higher caste status within it.

We see both these trends in the caste movements of Bombay and Madras. In Maharashtra Jyotiba Phule set up the Satyashodhak Samaj in 1873 to fight caste oppression and save "lower castes from the hypocritical Brahmans and their opportunistic scriptures". This movement struck roots among the pre-dominantly peasant Maratha castes. At another level it spread among villagers, taking on a more radical character which later inspired the peasant movement in Satara in 1919-21. The non-brahman movement in Maharashtra has a conti-nuity that can be traced through

Ambedkar and his Independent Labour party, the Republican Party of India after his death, the Dalit Panther movement of the early to mid 1970s and the Dalit assertion that fought for and won the renaming of Marathwada University to Ambedkar University last year.

In Madras the Justice movement launched around 1915-16 articulated the aspirations of the "intermediate" castes, which included numerous prosperous landlords and merchants, against the almost total Brahman domination in education, services and politics.

The movement developed an anti-caste system character in the late 1920s and early 1930s under the leadership of V. Ramaswamy Naicker, popularly known as Periyar. Periyar also flirted with socialism; and opened his journal to atheist and socialist writers. The non-brahman movement in Tamil Nadu was to an extent successful in destroying the Brahmanical hold over society and polity in the State.

The non-brahman movements also strengthened the first striving of nationality aspirations especially in Maharashtra, Tamil Nadu and Andhra Pradesh. They espoused the vernacular against Brahmanical Sanskrit, and in essence articulated their demands in regional terms. The anti-caste movements in the south were lent strength also because of the caste polarisation that exists in these regions. Brahmanical oppression enjoyed almost absolute and completely parasitical domination in these areas; that hold has largely (through regional variations still exists) been destroyed by these movements.

In the North the gradations of caste are more diverse. The pre dominance of the Brahmans in social economic and political power was relatively low. However the Unionist Party in Punjab was able to build a powerful agriculturist (i.e. landlord, and rich peasant) lobby including Jats and Muslims. In the Punjab, the Jats grew to dominate the entire society and culture and Brahmans were relegated to a secondary position.

In, Bihar in 1925 a government report talked of Yadavs "agitating for the improvement of social status of their caste" and it is important to note that the prominent kisan leader of the 1930s, Swami Sahajanand Saraswati began in the 1920s as an organiser of a Bhumihar Sabha. The Bhumihars in fact are originally a peasant caste in Bihar which successfully attained upper-caste status through a movement begun in this period. The Yadavs, Kurmis and Koeris also got together to organise a Triveni Sangh for upgradation of their status. The history of the peasant movement in the North in a sense marks the growing assertion of the large tenants who mainly come from the "intermediate" castes.

The struggles of the peasants against zimindari oppression also hid its inevitable effects on the caste system. The period since the second half of the nineteenth century, saw a large number of peasant movements breaking out in different parts of the country. Since zamindars were mainly upper-caste and tenants backward and lower castes, such struggles even though not articulated in caste terms, inevitably increased the upward mobility of the struggling tenants.

As mentioned earlier an upper caste and class bias in the leadership of the mainstream 'anti-colonial' movement prevented the assimilation of the non-Brahman movements. Gandhi's approach to tackle caste question was basically in terms of '*Harijan*' welfare. His campaigns were strictly limited to social reforms which were cosmetic in nature, delinking it from any economic demand. Gandhi refused to attack the caste system as a whole and in fact defended the original varna system. His reforms were basically a bid to establish hegemony over potentially more radical anti-caste movements from below.

The Caste System After 1947

The formal transfer of power of August 15, 1947, which basically was a compromise between the Indian ruling elites and their colonial masters, came as a 'great betrayal' to the aspirations of the millions of people who actively participated in the glorious struggles against colonialism. On the caste question also the safeguards built into the constitution by Dr Ambedkar, have been reduced to pious pronouncements. As Chairman of the drafting committee of the Constitution, Dr Ambedkar ensured that the abolition of untouchability and *begar*, the provision of reservations for Dalits in education, jobs and in Parliament, and allowing positive discrimination in favour of Dalits and "Backward Castes" was built into the Constitution. Through these provisions he hoped to arm the Dalits with political power, to improve their socio-economic and cultural conditions and realise their liberation from social stigma and caste oppression. Ambedkar also launched a bitter attack on brahmanical Hinduism as the basis of the caste system

Patriarchy and the Caste System

Brahmanical patriarchy is a structure unique to Hinduism of the caste order. It is a set of rules and institutions in which caste and gender are linked, each shaping the other and where the women are crucial in maintaining the boundaries of castes. Patriarchal codes in this structure ensure that the caste system can be reproduced without violating the hierarchical order of closed endogamous circles, each distinct from a higher and lower than others. Brahmanical codes for women differ according to the status of the caste group in the hierarchy of castes with the most stringent control over sexuality reserved as a privilege for the highest caste. It incorporates both an ideology of chaste wives and pativrata women who are valorised and a structure of rules and institutions by which caste he rarely and gender in equality are maintained through both the production of consent of the application of coercion.

The distinctive cultural signs for upper and lower caste women in terms of marriage and sexuality are also closely linked to the appropriation of the labour of the lower castes by the upper castes. This explains the ban on remarriage of upper caste women at one end and sometimes the enforced cohabitation of the lower caste women at the other. So caste system as a system of labour appropriation has shaped the codes of gender to further the ends of the upper castes.

So Brahmanical patriarchy is a mechanism to preserve land, women and ritual quality within it. The necessity of ensuring a labour supply to work on the land we can see that caste and patriarchy in the social formation of early India required not only a control of women's reproductive power of the upper caste through whom the closed structure of land and ritual quality was to be preserved but of all castes to ensure as generate labour supply. The lower caste male whose sexuality is a threat to upper caste purity of blood has to be institutionally prevented from having sexual access to women of the higher castes, so such women have to be carefully guarded.

The Literary perspective

I take up two literary works of great repute which describe in detail the trials and tribulations undergone by the dalits. The first work is U.R. Anantha Murthy's Samskara which is written in a revisionist and critical mode. Anantha Murthy is one of the few authors who have explicitly seemed to investigate in the system of caste hierarchy. I will try to show that his act of revision is partial as he stops while pointing to some of the ills of the brahmanical way of living and fails to indicate available alternatives. The author cannot envisage a role for oppressed people and sees no fault in the divisive system of caste. The other work is an autobiography by Omprakash Valmiki's Joothan. Joothan is taken up because it delivers a first hand account of a dalit's life. I focus on the level of narrative variation in these two novels. Samskara is originally a Kannada novel which was translated by A K Ramanujan in 1976. Joothan was originally written in Hindi and I refer to its English translation by Arun Prabha Mukherjee.

U.R. Anantha Murthy is one of the most important representatives of the new movement in the literature of the Kannada language and is counted among the most eminent Indian authors. The central themes in Anantha Murthy's literary production are the exploration of the caste system, religious rules and traditions as well as the ambivalent relationship between the handed down cultural value system and the new values of a changing world. Born in 1932 in the village of Melige in Karnataka, Anantha Murthy visited a traditional Sanskrit school there. He grew up, as he says, as a Gandhian socialist and later studied English and comparative literature in Mysore and Birmingham where, in 1966, he worked for his Ph.D. He was professor of English literature for several years at Mysore University, and later vice chancellor of the Mahatma Gandhi University in Kottayam, the chairman of the National Book Trust and President of the Sahitya Academy, the Indian Literature Academy.

Anantha Murthy began his literary career in 1955 with the story volume *Endendhigu Mugiyada Kathe*. Since then he has published four novels, one play, six short story volumes, five poetry volumes and six essay volumes in Kannada and several pieces of literature in English. His works have been translated into several Indian and European languages and have been awarded important literary prizes, including the Gyanpeeth Award (1994), the most renowned Indian literature prize. His most well-known novel is Samskara which was written in 1966. Samskara means "culture" as well as "ritual" but also means "death rites". It tells the story of a young Brahman-priest, Naranappa, who pays little attention to strict rules of the village community. When he dies of an epidemic, the village inhabitants refuse to do the funeral rites for him. But the predicament is that as long as he is not burned, they have to starve. The novel looks for the answer to the question: What is Samskara? Is culture only maintained if tradition is followed with blind fervour? Anantha Murthy tries to question discrimination through the caste system and the repressive belief practice of the brahmins in his other works also. In another novel Bharatipura (1973), he takes up an analogous theme in which a brahmin and land owner, Jagannatha, goes back to his home town which is bound strongly to caste, and tries to change the social structures there after his return from England. He wants to enable the untouchables to enter the temple, and with this, meets the resistance of the higher caste.

Anantha Murthy has engaged himself primarily with themes of social reform and review of the old traditions followed in society. But if his literary production, particularly Samskara, is put to the test of intensive reading, one can argue that his attack against the religious tradition of brahminism is largely superfluous and in fact he ends up in strengthening the same. If we compare the case of Anantha Murthy with that of Raja Rao, who is an out-and-out upholder of the tradition of brahminism, we may surprisingly not find major differences.

Anantha Murthy does not comment anything directly at the caste system but the ambience that he creates in his works clearly suggests his inclination towards the continuation of this tradition of brahmanism. His protagonist, Praneshacharya, in Samskara is said to have all the qualities of a brahmin. By contrasting the brahmanic Praneshacharya - his religiosity and respect for traditional values like devotion to God and respect for the institution of marriage with Naranappa, Anantha Murthy celebrates the caste system. Anantha Murthy's act of giving no space or recognition to the likes of Chandri, Naranappa'a mistress, suggests the writer's subtle advocacy of brahminism. All the Hindu Gods he mentions with reverence like Vishnu, Krishna and Rama are all protectors of this *dharma*. Anantha Murthy supports all that Raja Rao upholds in the name of 'Brahman'.

Anantha Murthy's two major characters, Naranappa and Praneshacharya, remain confused like Ramaswamy in The Serpent and the Rope. Both the brahmins appear to be average human beings as Naranappa surrenders his sense of religion for the carnal pleasures of life and Praneshacharya faces a strong dilemma to the very end whether to share his weaknesses with his fellow men or not.

The novel symbolises a clash of values represented by Naranappa and Praneshacharya. Naranappa belongs to the close-knit community of the Madhva brahmins. He lives in a brahmin village but eats meat, drinks and keeps a low-caste mistress, Chandri. Naranappa's rebellious behaviour is a source of intense resentment and hatred in the community. When he dies of the plague, no one is willing to cremate him. But as long as his body lies in the village, the brahmins are not allowed to touch food or water. No one dares touching Naranappa's sinful, contaminated corpse. As only a brahmin can cremate another brahmin, Chandri places all her jewellery at the feet of the leader of the community, Praneshacharya, for the expenses.

A seasoned brahmin scholar, an ascetic in his home where he tends his ailing wife, Praneshacharya is now faced with a moral problem. In order to lay their hands on the gold and end the pangs of hunger in their bellies, the brahmins suddenly vie with each other to cremate Naranappa. Praneshacharya spends a fruitless night pouring over the scriptures. In his dream he confronts the sneering Naranappa, reliving an encounter in real life, when he had failed to convince the self-proclaimed heretic of the righteousness of following God's path. He prays to Lord Maruti at the temple but the God gives no answer to his dilemma. Assailed by doubts, weary with starvation, he comes out of the temple to find Chandri waiting for him. When she falls at his feet, a subconscious need for the long denied warmth of a woman's body and the comfort from it makes him draw her into a closer embrace. Carried away by the passion of the moment, they make love in the night, violating all the codes that had so long held their society together. When no one can offer a solution to the problem of Naranappa's cremation, a group of Naranappa's drunken disciples, resolved to cremate their leader, come to his house the same night but are frightened away by the rats that infest the place. The whole village is swarming with rats carrying the plague from home to home. Women and children start leaving the village. Praneshacharya's wife dies and facing a personal dilemma, he too leaves the village. On his metaphorical pilgrimage, Praneshacharya befriends the gregarious low-caste, Putta, and comes to terms with the basic hypocrisy of his life. He comes back to the deserted village to cremate Naranappa himself in an act of expiation.

Though Anantha Murthy has questioned some aspects of social functioning, his idea of critiquing brahmanism appears hollow and holds no weight as he does not talk of an alternative paradigm of social behaviour and relations. The author has himself made it clear that he intends to interrogate the issue of caste which continues to haunt Indian society from times immemorial. The first aspect of my argument is that the text describes in great detail the lifestyle of the brahmins. The two most talked about characters (Naranappa and Praneshacharya) symbolise the brahmanic system. The novel presents detailed pictures of the village agrahara (clusters of houses in a village where Brahmins live) as to how do brahmins conduct themselves in their day to day life. Though Anantha Murthy is looking at the brahmanical domination with a revisionist approach, he does not see or assign any role for the marginalised sections. Naranappa and Praneshacharya prevail predominantly over the whole scenario and there are only oblique references to low-caste characters.

Nowhere in the novel we hear of the real feelings of Chandri, Belli, and Bhagirathi. Their voices seem to be insignificant. We do not know what they think of the Brahmin men nor do we know whether they felt exploited even at the hands of Praneshacharya because for all his goodness that he does represents the parasitic brahminism. The women, especially upper caste women, do not attack social system based on hierarchies but try to make the most from within its confines to their advantage even though they meet with resistance from their husbands and other male relatives. Brahmin male's liking for subaltern women is basically sexual gratification and a cruel weakness which invokes helplessness, exploitation and pain for the helpless females. The author does not pay attention to the psychosexual trauma that these women had to endure. It is not important enough for him and it appears that its occurrence is taken for granted. It is almost as though these women do not think about their sexual harassment. Crimes against subaltern women go unreported and are hardly considered seriously for it is they who are blamed for the problems that have been inflicted on them. If we consider the novel as being a part and product of the social set-up, then it also suffers from prevailing social evils and does not provide impetus to the spirit of progress and social reform. Those who are trapped inside the villages and agraharas of India are hardly given an occasion or opportunity to realise their plight and cause of it, this perhaps is more so, because the ostensible focus of the novel is Praneshcharya's consciousness that is reinforced by the powerful and recurrent use of socially sanctified myths. Praneshacharya's ordered life and his strict observance of rituals are all portrayed with a view to establish the atmosphere of tradition and custom imperative to Hindu Society. The novelist takes for granted the various Hindu myths and weaves his plot around them. Hindu-brahmanic ideas rather extended to all walks of his life, something which is respected by one and all in agrahara. The people in agrahara accept brahminism *per se* living happily in their well-defined life. Their habits, their emotions, their sentiments, in short their entire life is governed by the rituals of brahminism. They never attempt or indeed desire to challenge it. This is well brought out in the description of the events following Naranappa's death.

The caste system is world's largest surviving hierarchy and is based on the principle of purity and superiority, qualities that one is supposed to inherit by birth. A person becomes a member of a particular caste with his birth and dies in it. The dalits and low castes are outside the caste system and their exploitation is a general feature throughout India. They are looked down upon because of their low caste; birth in a low caste is supposed to be the result of their bad deeds or *karma*. If caste system had to be done away with, Naranappa would have been given a decent funeral and Praneshacharya would not have had as close an encounter with Chandri as he had. Praneshacharaya's case also gets worse with caste rules as, if we analyse it from within the Hindu caste system or else, he could have easily married Chandri following his wife's death. Therefore, throughout the novel, caste comes out as a defining feature of Samaskara and its shadow continues to haunt all the characters. Not one character his entire novel can think beyond caste nor can he or she, attempts to destroy it. Caste system has survived because of the security that it sometimes provides people occupying superior positions. It is the internalisation of brahmanical ideas that moves the characters. Chandri does not know her way out after violation of the norms of the Hindu society. After performing Naranappa's cremation with the aid of Muslims, she does not know which way to go. The point is that Chandri is made to think within the tyrannical Hindu-brahmanical system and is unable to break free. She is not allowed to have any autonomy. The little autonomy that she achieves is when she walks out of caste norms.

Another, aspect of caste based discrimination which Samskara presents before us is related with the taboos which prohibit a brahmin to eat food touched/prepared by a member of a lower caste. Religious documents like the Vashistha Dharma Sutra specify what may be eaten and what may not. It stipulates that a brahmin can not consume anything from a Sudra. The caste hierarchies accept and encourage a rigid structure of social inequality – the greater one's purity, or lack of contact with pollution, the higher one's rank. Dasacharya, one of the brahmins in the novel, is afraid of social criticism, if he openly eats food at Manjayya's place. Being a smarta, Manjayya is considered to belong to a lower sect of brahmins. Dasacharya is afraid that if he eats "cooked stuff in a smarta house" (57), he may be boycotted by his own sect, "I do not really mind eating in your house but if those rascals in our agrahara hear about it, no one will invite me to a ceremony again. What can I do Manjayya?" When Manjayya amusedly assured him of secrecy, Dasacharya ask for some milk, jaggery and flat-rice. Secretly delighted that an agrahara brahmin had come to eat with them, his wife gleefully serves. Naranappa, before he dies, does not practice such discrimination, yet Chandri is unable to come to terms with such unorthodox behaviour. She repeatedly requests him to not eat food cooked by her (45). The readers get the feeling that society could perhaps pardon Naranappa for having a close relationship with a low caste prostitute but not the fact that he ate what Chandri cooked is still a graver sin. Lakshmana's statement, in which he lays emphasis on the fact that he, in addition to having a mistress, even ate food cooked by her, makes it amply clear.

It is believed that contact with a person of lower caste can alter one's purity and may require some form of remedial procedure such as taking a bath or changing clothes. When Chandri calls at Praneshcharya's home to inform him about Naranappa's death, he is yet to take his meal. The readers are told how he will have to bathe again to purify himself if he talks to Chandri before taking his food: "If the Acharya talked to her, he would be polluted; he would have to bathe again before his meal" (2). Being a traditional brahmin, Praneshacharya has been conditioned not to eat food cooked or served by a person who belongs to a lower caste. It is a commonly followed practice as other people know and respect this constraint.

In the course of the novel, Putta takes the Acharya to a brahmin restaurant for coffee, telling him that they keep a special place inside for orthodox brahmins like him. Still fearing the presence of some familiar person, the Acharya is worried as it may have a ripple effect later on, if "someone sees the crest jewel of Vedanta philosophy drinking a cup of polluted restaurant coffee" (115). Afraid of entering a temple and eating there during the period of his wife's mourning, he realises that he would never have the courage to defy brahmin practices as Naranappa had done (116).

Many anthropologists have remarked on the critical importance of pollution to the caste system. A non-brahmin, particularly a *shudra*, an untouchable, is never considered clean enough either to share food with a brahmin, or even touch him. When Chandri requests Sheshappa, the cartman, to cremate Naranappa's body, he refuses: "Chandravva that can not be done. Do you want me to go to hell, meddling with a brahmin corpse? Even if you give me all eight kinds of riches, I can't" (69-70). the internalisation of caste hierarchies can also be seen in Putta's attempts to climb the caste ladder by denying the social background of his mother. He tells Praneshacharya that he is a Malera; his mother belonged to a lower caste and was not married to his father who was a high-class brahmin. He flaunts the sacred thread and claims that all his buddies are brahmin boys (112).

Samskara presents a vivid picture of a society which has accepted caste discrimination as a norm. Anantha Murthy accepts that without question. His novel has unquestioningly accepted brahmin eminence and pushed the lower caste people to the margins where they cease to have any significance. The brahmins are supposed to be the spiritual and temporal guides, teachers and exponents of law, whereas the *shudras* perform menial services only. They are refused even the semblance of equality. Their hutments are quite a distance away from the brahmin agrahara (39). The abject poverty of their life is also discernible. They depend on manual labour for their livelihood. Chinni and Belli pick up cow dung. They are treated with indifference. Chinni begs for something to eat, standing at a distance from a brahmin woman, "please, avva, throw a morsel for my mouth, avva" (58). Betel leaf, betel nut and tobacco are thrown at her from some distance. Such an incident, on the one hand, highlights the extent of untouchability practiced in Indian society, and on the other, projects the dalit characters without any initiative and substance. The issue of representation is raised by many dalit writers, philosophers and theorists. They believe that all literature by non-dalit writers having dalits as characters does not do justice to their identity. If at all they find a mention, they are systematically reduced to an insignificant set of bones, without brains. This is done without exception even when dalits perform some of the most important activities at all levels. In real society, dalits are the ones who do all hard work in agricultural fields and factories and contribute significantly to the working of the Indian nation.

The closed character and inescapability of caste also comes out in Samskara. Naranappa who had violated all the taboos propagated and fostered by the brahmanic culture of the agrahara continues to be a brahmin till the end of his life. He cannot be treated like an outcaste and "remains a brahmin in his death" (9).

He had sneered at the Praneshacharya and all his brahmin ways during his life. He had refused to marry a relative as is ordained by custom. He had wanted to roll up all brahmanic respectability and "throw it always for a little bit of pleasure with one female" (21). He took his Muslim friends to the Ganapati temple stream and caught the sacred free-swimming and trusting fish. Even after his gross neglect and violations of all traditional norms, the brahmins do not want any non-brahmin to touch his dead body as this may invite wrath from the heavens.

Praneshacharya who embodies a virtuous facet of the traditional brahmanic cult proves to be an ordinary person in the end as he cannot resist the temptations of ordinary life. Even in his period of wandering and deviation, he is approached by a villager who requests him to read 'a bit of future' (95). Praneshacharya also recognises this when he was about to perform the routine brahmin functions by sheer habit, reigns himself suddenly and ruefully ponders that one can not run away from one's caste: "Even if I leave everything behind, the community cling to me, asking to fulfill duties the brahmin is born to" 96).

The voices of all marginalised sections (women, outcastes) are weak and incoherent babble. The significant point is that Chandri, a lower caste woman, who possesses the profundities and complexities of a human mind and also an acute practical sharpness, has not received positive attention. Even against all odds, she tries to arrange Naranappa's cremation. When Sheshappa indicates his inability to meddle with a brahmin corpse, she seeks the help of a Muslim acquaintance. Without bothering for religious rituals, she carries the corpse to the cremation ground and burns it. Praneshacharya, the high priest, retains his superior place, his stature remains undiminished and the author seems to sympathise with him a great deal. Praneshacharya's logic is based on an otherworldly and mysterious rationale of religion and his method of taking decisions is at times based on blind chance, as he does much to his approval of the other brahmins of the agrahara and surrounding areas like placing of flowers on Maruti's shoulders.

But within the novel, only the oppressed sections come under attack and Praneshacharya is venerated for believing in obscurantism. This presumptuous understanding of the Hindu faith results in a false consciousness that goes against all subaltern sections, leads the hierarchy to gain mastery and control of the ostensibly recalcitrant others. Naranappa's logic that is based on his discrete understanding of the selected myths and Hindu treatises is treated as a false consciousness even though it presents a radical understanding of the Hindu view of life and is definitely more modern and broadminded. Any logic that goes against the established order and its norms or is inimical to its chosen ends becomes an object that has to be attacked. Whatever Naranappa says is subordinated by brahmins by pointing an accusing finger at his philistinism and disregard for sanctioned behaviour for the Madhava males. His engagements are never refuted with counter logic but merely brushed aside and condemned. Matters are always seen from the selective lens of religion which is consistent with brahminism. When Naranappa says that Lakshmana is so greedy that "he will even lick a copper coin off a heap of shit," (24) he portrays the real weakness of brahmins for money. Through Naranappa, Anantha Murthy demolishes the myths surrounding brahmins by criticising their greed for money and gold but also for the marriages which are arranged not so much according to the ruling stars, or on the bases of *gunas* in the horoscopes but for economic gains. The author makes it clear that it is not Naranappa who is degenerated but the rest of the brahmin community. Most of the brahmins portrayed in the novel are hypocritically selfish, greedy, narrow-minded and even short-sighted, who take shelter behind the ancient Hindu classics, its high sounding principles and the traditional morality which serve as masks to hide their contemptible self. Not surprisingly, the entire agrahara throws brickbats at Naranappa after his death, something they were unable to do when he was alive. In the words of Lakshmana-charya:

I am not the sort who would hide anything about him just because he was my close relative. He was my wife's uncle's son. We tolerated him and sheltered him in our lap as long as we could. In return, what does he do? He comes to the river in full view of all the Brahmins and takes the holy stones that we have worshipped for generations and throws it in the river and spites after it. Condone everything if you wish – but didn't he, willfully before our eyes, bring Muslims over and in the wide open frontyard, eat and drink forbidden things? If any of us questioned him, in good faith, he would turn on us, cover us with abuse from head to foot. As long as he lived, we just had to walk in fear of him.(7)

It is noteworthy that these socalled high class groups flex their muscles only when the disobedient and the outcast brahmin Naranappa is no more. This also shows the weakness of their belief, their fear and their lack of firmness.

Praneshcharya's thinking undergoes a seachange after his sexual contact/intercourse with Chandri. His single track mind starts seeing not just the light of God but shades that are inescapable for ordinary mortals. It is his acceptance of the more controversial side of life that his religion negates, and his subsequent attempts to come to grips with his own situation, that makes him a truly credible character: It is the honesty with which he tries to come to grapple with his own inner self that makes him a likable personality. After all, he did indulge in sexual activities that neither his station in the Madhava community nor his religion could ever approve. In our eyes he does not fall as a man because he does not try cheating himself with falsehoods:

He remembered the first maxim of yoga, "yoga is the stilling of the waves of the mind". "But No!', "put aside even the consolation of recitations and God's holy names, stand alone," He said to himself. May the mind be like the patterns of light and shade, the forms of branching trees give naturally to sunshine, light in the sky, shadow under the trees, patterns on the ground. If, luckily, there's spray of water – rainbows. May one's life be that sunshine. A mere awareness, a sheer astonishment, still, floating still and self-content like the sacred brahmini-kite in the sky (91).

As mentioned earlier, there is a clear shift in Praneshacharya's thoughts after his experience with Chandri and his wanderings. He realises after witnessing the cock-fight with Putta that "one part of lust is tenderness; the other part is a demoniac will." (22) The sexual experience for him is so overpowering that it becomes a manifest dream in which there is a simultaneous production of past and present that fantasises the future. It is the pull of sex, all that his own wife Bhagirathi lacked, that suspends his rational faculties. It is not Chandri that he fantasises about. It is Belli. The uncanny fusion of terror and excitement is the insoluble dilemma that he must enact or die. The erotogenic pleasures arise in the middle of the prolonged death scenes, be it Naranappa or a bird. It is not just Chandri but "Belli's earth-coloured breasts"; if there are thoughts of Bhagirathi 'the alter of his sacrifice', he also cherishes the prospects of sleeping with Padmavati. Thus, we can say that just like an ordinary human being and unlike the "crest jewel of Vedanta Philosophy", Praneshcharya's sexuality due to repression knows know no bounds once it is given a free play.

It is not only in this creative work that all the subaltern voices are subordinated; history is filled with such instances. In fact, there is a systematic effort to do so in the writing of history. The marginalisation of dalits in Samskara is quite in keeping with the historical biases and tradition. What Gramsci had to say about their lack of a collective identity is true for our purposes also because the subalterns fail to rally behind Chandri or others whenever they are pitted against the brahmins. The precondition for strength is their being unified or attaining a collective dominant position which the brahmins would not allow. The fever of brahminism loosened by Naranappa's death imposes itself on the subalterns and the 'temperature curves' of the high born lower only when they have castigated the subalterns with full-throated ease. Naranappa's funeral causes a rupture between the past and the present and helps refigure their wisdom in the middle of the plague. The dissent embodied by the presence of Muslims, with received thought becomes an attempt to question the tyranny of sacrosanct and arbitrary brahmin thought. The lower castes or subalterns are treated like objects which need constant surveillance by the brahmins. Chandri's initiative in Naranappa's cremation is significant and path-breaking as it is an enabling step for other subalterns – it is revolutionary for the reason that it hints towards a contestion of the brahmins.

The brahmin and lower caste communities are a segregated lot although crossing of borders does take place off and on. Whenever this happens, the latter are exploited. Attempts are made to absorb the subalterns within the brahmin economy by reducing them to servitude and by grabbing their meagre possessions. The lower castes in the novel never attack the brahmins verbally or by use of force. The novel connives in stereotypical subjectification of the people figuring down below in the caste-hierarchy, though Chandri appears to be an exception as her challenging decision about the funeral symbolises the subaltern's latent capacity for activist ingenuity. Their fragmented identities are taken advantage of by Hinduism's patriarchs against whom Chandri unwittingly plays the role of a subversive agency. Not many critical opinions are in her favour as not many critics have weighed her beyond her role as a prostitute. The novel does not provide any space to her or help her conceptualise any alternative form of sociality. Putta, by harping on his father being a Brahmin, tries to foist an alternative genealogy in terms of Hindu logic and thinking. Therefore, within Samskara, the subalterns appear as a broken people, partially because of their lack of any homogeneity, for there are categories and divisions among the subalterns/dalits also.

There is a fundamental difference between dalit and non-dalit writers and thinkers in the ways they analyse and interpret various facets of society and history. On the subject of representing the dalit voice, non-dalit authors are either hesitant or merely sympathetic. The sheer anguish that the dalit community has experienced historically is missing in their narratives and stories. As Omprakash Valmiki writes:

> Dalit life is excruciatingly painful, charred by experiences. Experiences that did not manage to find room in literary creations. We have grown up in a social order that is extremely cruel and inhuman and compassionless towards dalits. (Joothan, Preface)

'Joothan' literally means scraps of food left on a plate, destined for the garbage or for the family pet in a middle-class urban home. It is related to the word 'jootha', which means polluted and such scraps are characterised as 'joothan' only if someone else eats them. surprisingly, there exists no eqvivalent word in the English language. India's Untouchables have been forced to accept and eat 'joothan' for their subsistence for centuries. The word encapsulates the pain, humiliation and poverty of this community, which has lived at the bottom of India's social pyramid for millennia. Although untouchability was legally abolished in the constitution of the newly independent India in 1949, dalits continue to be threatened by discrimination, economic deprivation, violence and ridicule.

Dalit autobiographies basically constitute a challenge to this institutional narrative by presenting what they claim are 'factual' experiences of untouchability from the writer's own life. Valmiki, for instance, does this by repeatedly narrating his experiences of pain as exclusion due to the continued practice of untouchability. He writes, "I was kept out of extracurricular activities. On such occasions I stood on the margins like a spectator. During the annual functions of the school, when rehearsals were on for the play, I too wished for a role. But I always had to stand outside the door. The so-called descendents of the gods cannot understand the anguish of standing outside the door" (16). In another instance, Valmiki relates how he was continually kept out of the chemistry lab 'on some pretext or the other and despite protesting to the head master of the school, nothing was done to enforce the equality of every student. He writes, "Not only did I do poorly in the lab tests in the board exam, I also got low marks in the oral, even though I had answered the examiners questions quite correctly" (133-34).

The conclusive assessment of this paper is that caste-system has an all-pervading influence on Indian society. The society that U.R. Anantha Murthy presents in his novels is influenced by the caste-system but this important insight has not received any critical attention so far. There is a fundamental chasm between dalit and non-dalit authors and activists in their ways of analysis of different facets of our society and history. All dalit authors are trying to point towards a systematic design behind the total absence of the dalit perspective in mainstream literature and by the absolute necessity of bringing these points of views into operation with the dominating Hindu narratives of Indian history, society, nationalism and colonialism.

Bibliography

Anantha Murthy, U R. Samskara (Tr. A.K. Ramanujan), OUP, 1976; New Pub Ed., 1989.

Gaikwad, Laxman. The Branded Trans (Uchlaya) Sahitya Akademi: New Delhi, 1998.

Rao, Raja. *The Serpent and the Rope*. Orient: New Delhi, 1968.

Rao, Raja. *The Chess Master and His Moves*. Vision: New Delhi, 1988.

Rao, Raja. *The Meaning of India*. Vision: New Delhi, 1996.

Valmiki, O P. *Joothan*. Columbia University Press: New York. 2003.

Guru, Gopal. '*Dalits in Pursuit of Modernity*', India: Another Millennium? (Ed), Romila Thapar. Viking, 2000.

Guru, Gopal. '*The Language of Dalit-Bahujan Political Discourse*' in Dalit Identity and Politics. (Ed.) G. Shah. Sage: New Delhi, 2001.

Habib, Irfan. Essays in Indian History: Towards a Marxist Perception. Tulika: Delhi, 1995.

Hanlon, Rosalind O'. *Caste, Conflict and ideology*: Mahatma Jotirao Phule and low caste protest in nineteenth-century western India. Cambridge University Press, 1985.

Heehs, P. Nationalism, *Terrorism, Communalism. Essays in Modern Indian History*. OUP: New Delhi. 1997.

Hertzler, Joyce O. *The Social Thought of The Ancient Civilisations*. McGraw: New York, 1936.

Hinndls, John and Eric Sharpe. *Hinduism, Newcastle upon Tyne*, Oriel Press, 1972.

Hobsbawm, Eric. *The Invention of Tradition*, ed. Eric Hobsbawm and Terence Ranger Cambridge: Cambridge U P, 1989.

Ilaiah, Kancha. *Why I am Not a Hindu: a Shudra critique of Hindutva Philosophy*, Culture and Political Economy. Samya: Calcutta, 1996

Jafferlot, Christopher. *Hindu Nationalism: Strategic Syneretic in Ideology Building*, EPW, March 20, 1993.

Jayal, Neeraja Gopal. (Ed) Democracy in India. Oxford University Press: Oxford, 2001.

14

Margins of Print: Dalit in Nation, Region and Print Culture

Ranjith Thankappan

Introduction

This paper looks at Dalit debates in the Malayalam speaking region- Keralam- by locating it at the narrative praxis of literary/journalistic/print culture as represented in some of the literary spaces and the journalistic space of Dalit little magazines. The attempt is to understand the latent socio-cultural process which shapes the community formation among Dalits in the sub-national space of a post-colonial region known as Kerala, the southernmost Indian state. The assumption is that such an inquiry into Dalit discourses of the region would reflect upon the nuances of socio-cultural transformation taking place in society, the locus point being the structural power relations centred on the institution of caste.

In the Indian context, Dalit, the historically marginalised 'untouchable' social group, posses the political potential of a socio-cultural transformation as its evolution into a political community could challenge the existing hegemonies. The conceptualisation of such a community should happen from within and should be self-reflecting and politically engaging. The modality of such an evolution engages the ideological dispositions of various agency narratives such as that of Indian state, Hindu community discourse, Dalitmovement and academic discourse. This process also imbibes energy from the history of social movements/struggles and contemporary social/cultural/political realities.

Here, I would limit my engagement with the debates in the narrative praxis of the print cultural practices of Dalits and its cultural connotations in the context of emerging community assertions. The debates taking place in the literary and journalistic narrative spaces are signifiers to the evolving cultural discourses that shape the aspirations and consciousness leading to the imagination of the community and vice versa. The paper is arranged in two parts. First part will discuss the social/cultural/political context that makes it imperative to look into these discourses and the second part where these print narratives are interrogated and interpreted so as to contribute theoretically to the discourse.

The vantage point into these cultural debates demands the subjective interventions from within the community. The category 'Dalit' has been used here not as a homogenous category, but that works within a caste hierarchical, class conscious and gendered system constructing multiple levels of power relations. However, in order to pose itself as a counter hegemonic value system 'Dalit' strives to address all these aspects at the deepest possible level. That is the "potential", I see in this historically driven and politically conscious cultural category.

Modernity, Dalits and Region: The Context

The critical engagements of Dalits with modernity and nation have been one of the sites of socio-political leapfrogging in the last six decades of independent India. The Dalit discourse always tried to interrogate the question of nation at various levels of socio-cultural milieu. This has been contested by the nationalists as 'deviant', 'sectarian', 'casteist' and as a 'side issue', or 'something insignificant'[1] that could be addressed after the political question of sovereignty of nation. The imagination of nation has masked the whole discourse and Dalits have challenged this hegemonic construct of nation at various historical junctures. The discourses dealing with the question of equality, citizenship, cultural plurality, right to cultural/political/economic resources etc. were fundamental to the Dalit discourse on nation.

The nation was built on the pillars of a modernist's tryst with the past. The Nehruvian development agenda that carved out the notion of a modern nation-state aping a western secular model of nation, hesitate to address the internal struggles of a newly imagined national community. The offerings of colonial past that paved the path for the construction of nation-state had been denied to the vast majority of the population in the name of nationalism. The modern temples of development were built on the subjugated aspirations of a culturally complex social system. It was critiqued from various ideological and socio-political milieus. The hegemonic denominations built on a Hindu revivalist rightist ideology seen it as threat posed by modernity to tradition. The myth of secular development has been contested and attempt was made to re-impose traditional cultural values in the public realm via political rhetoric, institutions, print and visual media, etc.[2]

On the other hand, there seems to be the emergence of a critique of modernity from Dalit/Adivasi/women/minority Muslim positions. Dalit/Adivasi/Women's politics had problematised the grand narratives of modernity, at the same time, critically assimilating and strategically negotiating with its offerings. This critique need not be misinterpreted and limited to the traditional discomforts with modernity. Its re-emergence in the recent history could be traced to the historical evolution of identity movements across the globe. Its context in India has been politically narrated by the collapse of Soviet Union in late 80s, growth of rightist Hindu revivalism, demolition of Babri Masjid, changes in global politics in the context of Kuwait and Iraq wars etc.[3] However, the genealogy of a Dalit/subaltern critique could be historically traced back to Mahatma Phule, Ambedkar, Ayyankali and various anti-caste movements in the particular regional context. Aditya Nigam (2000) views the emergent Dalit critique of modernity as an 'absent presence' in the large body of Dalit writings and espouses a new theoretical framework to look at critically the modern political institution of nation.[4]

The emergence of new discourses from the shadows of grand narratives has occupied the centre stage of the renewed realm of political thought and activism. The (unwritten) micro histories of nation challenged the notion of the 'universal' and bring to light the multiculturalism and plurality that grows beyond the binaries of good/bad, mass/class, high art/low art etc. However, the influence of grand narratives on the outcome of nation remained the same. The status quos in the power structure was maintained and adhered to with the renewed neo-conservative enthusiasm. Modernist engagements and its narrative contracts were extended to retain the traditional power positions on nation. These critiques of Nehruvian modern nation point to the limitations of the grand narratives of secularism and nationalism.

The private realms of the society remained 'traditional' in essence and the public realms ushered in the glories and gains of modernity. Modern nation with its federal wings and new cultural artifacts was built in heterogeneous times of modernity. Press as a cultural artifact and democratising instrument played a major role in the process. The scope of print capitalism was extended to journalism which later grown as a post-colonial capitalist and corporate enterprise with the neo-liberal facet. It is by making a claim on nation that communities began to engage with the modern institution of nation-state. During the colonial era various communities based on the institution of caste and religion began asserting their identity and attempted to intervene the colonial discourse on nation. Representation of these various communities vis-à-vis caste, religion, gender was central to these debates. Many contemporary political discourses could also be traced back to these colonial debates.

As Stuart Blackburn (2006) points out that "no scholar can ignore the influence of print, especially its power to cast oral traditions in new forms, to new audiences, across linguistic and geographical boundaries."[5] The press acts as an instrument in constructing the debates in contemporary history. It helped communities to imagine and reach out to each and every member of the community via opinion leaders. As communities began asserting politically, the press became the tool to disseminate their angst and aspirations to all its members. The print became a tool to imagine an identity for the community. The dominant community imaginations could translate the idea of community into that of nation thereby acquire cultural supremacy.

Locating the Debate within Kerala

Kerala attained statehood with the linguistic re-organisation of states on 1st November 1956. As a region, it has culturally evolved out of various socio-political movements that envisaged and experienced the ideals of modernity. The print culture has played a prominent role in defining this society. The influence that various community\caste organisations had on this process also cannot be overlooked. The conflicting community\caste aspirations together with the nationalist discourse had defined the region, the backdrop of which was the spirit of Renaissance brought forth by various social reform movements. Arunima (2006) has pointed out that the naming of the region and people residing there- Kerala and Malayali- occurred "as a result of the complex negotiation between different community identities and different kinds of 'selves'. The fragility of this nascent 'Malayali' self is the one that found voice in the early literary prose genres."[6]

In the olden days, Kerala was a place of imagined boundaries and constraints- boundaries on where particular people might go; constraints on what they might do.[7]The institutionalised form of caste system in Kerala was so inhuman and rigid that it treated the 'lower' castes as not only as 'untouchable' but also as 'unseeble'. It was this barbaric nature of the caste oppression in Kerala that made Swami Vivekananda lament that the Kerala was a 'lunatic asylum'. The fact that the Keralam was one of the most caste-ridden parts of India has been agreed by scholars from different disciplines.[8] Noted historian K.N.Panikker(1995) observes this as:

"The subservience of 'lower' castes was manifest in all realms of social intercourse. A Nayar could not touch a Nambudiri, a Thiyya [or Ezhava] had to keep at least 32 feet away from him, and a Cheruma 64 feet. Even the style of conversation indicated the superior\inferior status. The violation of these rules led to excommunication- the denial of village services like those of a barber or washer-man and the facilities of village temples and wells."[9]

Over the years, Kerala has overcome these barriers and become a developmental model, popularly known as Kerala Model of Development. This model has a phenomenal influence upon the development discourse of post-colonial India. It is a model of development that envisages high level of social progress without recourse to economic growth. Gemma Cairo (2001) has analysed the influence and pressure that various social groups had exerted on the state in order to fulfill their interests and the ways that in turn produced the Kerala's distributive model.

However, the claims of 'Kerala Model' have been contested by the struggles of various Dalit\subaltern groups in the region. The Dalit and Women scholars have been attempting to theorise these movements and a coherent body of Dalit/Women's critique of the 'Kerala Model of Development' has evolved.[10]Whenever there was a general improvement in socio-economic conditions, the Dalits heaved a sigh of relief But within the social structure their status remained the same. K. Kunhaman (2002) points out:

"...in the intellectual marginalisation of the Dalits and Adivasis, Kerala seems to have out-performed the other Indian states... while they have got some access to general higher education, they are terribly under-represented in professional and technical education...There are no Dalit\Adivasi among top ranking journalists, scientists, technologists or university Vice-Chancellors. Thus, social discrimination and intellectual untouchablity are very strong, perhaps stronger than in any other states in India." [11]

The cultural and political discourse of the region has been largely carried forward by caste/religious aspirations. But the social public domain remains dominated by the rhetoric of class determinism, masking the modern cultural evolution of caste and religion. Dalit assertions on the other hand are ambiguously divided and therefore, inadequately represented in the political domain. The apolitical caste\sub-caste organisations by and large, function as patriarchal\revivalist groups ideologically confined within the umbrella of Hinduism. The emerging Dalit intelligentsia in the state has shown the courage to dethrone the hegemonic ideals of Hinduism and is in the process of re-writing history from a Dalit perspective, theoretical platforms of which are yet to evolve.

The land reforms in Kerala, initiated on December 8, 1957, by the first communist government in Kerala and 'completed' on January 1, 1970, with the official abolition of feudalism, had given land-ownership only to the non-Dalit tenants who were middle-men between the landlords and the labourers.[12] The Dalits were also kept away from the cultural realm as the dominant Malayali culture pertains to be that of the 'upper' castes.

Kerala is a state with highest proliferation of newspapers and magazines. Jeffrey has pointed out that the even in the early decade of 20th century many Malayalam newspapers and magazines had high circulation. The reading culture that was nourished within the interface of journalism and print cultures helped the region to carve a niche out of the ordinary modes through which such a media space developed in other parts of the country. The emerged scholarship on the concept of region points to the linkages of vernacularisation of public sphere vis-à-vis print capitalism with the emergence of linguistic regions.

Rich Freeman (2006) argues that the in relation to identity formation, literature as a special kind of reflexive language practice enables communities in creating and indexing various sorts of cultural capital and cultural identity, both regional and trans-regional. Anderson's hypothesis that print culture fostered the formulation of the myth of a past and geographic and ethnic community that replaced a sense of extra-territorial religious community may not be applicable to all the South Asian contexts. However, the expansion of print culture and its use by individuals who did not belong to the original secular elite encouraged the diffusion of new multiple conceptions of extra-territorial communities, however "nationalist" they may or may not have been.[13] What I am trying to argue, in this paper is that the neo-literate engagements of Dalits offer the possibilities of re-imaging a community beyond the statist hegemonic construct. The questions that arise are: (i) do Dalits as community possesses the agency to narrate its 'Self'? (ii) how far the political identity of Dalits been transformed into the cultural terrain? (iii) Do literary practice enable them to acquire the print capital and will it catalyse the process of community formation among Dalits?

The print culture of the region has addressed these questions as part of colonial literary consciousness and discourse, eventually carved out of the grant narratives of modernity. The early Malayalam novels such as *Saraswativijayam* (by Potheri Kunjambu, 1893), *Ghatakavadham* (Mrs. Collins, 1865) advocated religious conversion as an agency for solving these problems of tradition placing it within the ambit of colonial modernity. The critique of such a discourse could be seen in the emerging Dalit cultural debates made visible by various literary and print engagements of Dalits. Though 'Dalit' had occupied thematic centrality of early Malayalam literature, the Dalit as a writer arrived only in the literary horizon of 1960s.[14] The contemporary political significance of print for Dalit lies in the emergence of this new category – Dalit writer/intellectual- which has inaugurated the cultural moment of political modernity through which Dalits articulate their agency.

Dalits have tried in vain to assay forth this hegemonic cultural sphere with their own cultural practices. These attempts, by and large reflect the conflicts and commotion among the Dalits of Kerala in addressing the politics of asserting one's identity. And it is through these debates that Dalits attempt to re-define their identity and construct the 'Self' of a community.

Margins of Print: Dalits and Community

The Dalit interrogations of caste experiences in the region re-invoke the dialogue on nation and nation-state. The orientalist gaze of colonial modernity and the governmentality of national modernity tried to co-opt the emancipatory project of the marginalised. The print culture has been one of the contested spaces for the marginalised in various regions to engage critically with these projects.

The process of community formation among Dalits offers not a linear narrative as imagined by the nationalist or Indian state. On the contrary, it brings forth complex and multilayered narrative which at times could be contradicting as well. The problematising of structural inequalities in Indian society could not be effective unless one addresses the nuances in the process of community formation among Dalits. It could brings forth the internal tensions and strategic negotiations that various narratives and historical junctures possibly. The temporal and tangible terrains of the process demand a new theoretical perspective.

The recurring themes of these print narratives bring forth the latent process of constructing an unbound seriality through its print narratives.[15] This constructed unboundedness helps the community imagines the self in a particular fashion. However, these narratives also rely heavily on the dominant notions that define the whereabouts of nation and provide access to it in order to make a claim. These narratives are centred on certain debates that shape the identity of Dalits as a community such as the issue of reservation, Hindu religion, religious conversion, identity, caste and gender. It could be seen that the differing ideological positions bring forth a multi-layered narrative. The anger of young community members could be seen in these writings. They urge the community to take a pro-active role to fight the casteist/brahminical exclusionary measures of the public domain and create their own spaces within this sphere by utilising any possible means.

Conclusion

The complexities involved in the formation of a socially constructed, culturally perceived and politically articulated community of Dalits could be seen in these print narratives. Though placed in the hetero-normative and gender-problematic cultural terrain, the debates emanating from the narrative praxis of these magazines envisages a renewed political translation of culture vis-à-vis the lived experiences of the Dalit/subaltern. It demands a new theoretical approach and agency to the downtrodden. I was trying to map some of the visible facets of these debates and argue that; (a) the process of community formation among Dalits is a complex one and may not confine to a linear and monolithic understanding and theorisation; (b) the categories placed as binaries such as oppressor/oppressed, Dalit/brahman, male/female, hetero/homo etc may not be the only sources of knowledge production to address the political question of Dalit emancipation. Though culture is practiced within the framework of opposing binaries, its complexity also needs to be addressed. While addressing the binaries one should be able to see the conflation of various floating identities that determine and contextualise the political/cultural/social outcomes; (c) print engagement of Dalits is part of a historical continuity which necessitates the expansion of the newly emerged cultural terrain to other media forms and various cultural practices. (d) These are invisible in the mediated and caste-constituted Indian public/media sphere. However, the politics of community assertions/formations of Dalits assay forth as an emancipatory project that challenges both the grand narratives of tradition and modernity, at the same time negotiating with the latter in order to overcome the hurdles posed by the existing structural inequalities.

Notes

1. See Thirumal, P. (1997), "State Media and National Culture" in Dua M. R. and Manonmani (Ed.) *Communication and Culture: New Perspectives and Applications.* pp. 10-13 and Rajagopal, Aravind (2005) *Politics After Television.*

2. See M.S.S. Pandian (1998), "Stepping Outside History? New Dalit Writings from Tamil Nadu" in *Wages of Freedom: Fifty Years of the Nation-state*.
3. For a detailed discussion see Aditya Nigam (2000). Also see Meera Nandna (2001) and V. Geetha (2001) for the critique of Aditya Nigam's essay in *Economic and Political Weekly.*
4. Stuart Blackburn (2006), p. 1.
5. G.Arunima (2006), "Imagining Communities-differently : Print, language and the 'Public Sphere' in colonial Kerala", *The Indian Economic and Social History Review*, 43, 1.
6. Jeffrey, Robin 1992, p. 19.
7. Krishna Iyer, L.A. (1970), EMS (1968), Jeffrey, Robin (1992), Panikker, K.N. (1995).
8. Panikker, K.N., 1998, p. 180.
9. See the writings of Baburaj, Sunny Kapikkadu, K.K. Kochu, G. Raghu, Rekharaj etc.
10. Kunhaman, M. (2002), *Globalisation A Subaltern Perspective.* pp. 101-102.
11. K.K. Koch (2008), "Oru Aldaivathinte Maranam" (Death of a Godman), *Mathrubhumi* weekly, April 6-12.
12. See review by Smith, Charles D. He points towards the complexities involved in the process of imagining nation and nationalism while reviewing the essay "Imagined Identities, Imagined Nationalisms: Print Culture and Recent Scholarship" by Israel Gershoni and James P. Jankowski, *Redefining the Egyptian Nation* 1930-1945.
13. Benedict Anderson, *Imagined Communities*. Also see Partha Chatterjee, *Anderson's Utopia.*

Select Bibliography

Aloysius, G. 1998. *Nationalismwithout a Nation in India:* New Delhi: OxfordUniversity Press.

Anderson, Benedict. 1983. *Imagined Communities:Reflection on the Origin and Spread of Nationalism.* London: Verso.

Arunima, G. 2006. *Imagining Communities – Differently: Print, Language and the 'Public Sphere' in Colonial Kerala. The Indian Economic and Social History Review* 43 (1) (2006): pp. 63-76.

Blackburn, Stuart. 2003.*Print, Folklore and Nationalism in Colonial South India.* New Delhi: Permanent Black.

Chatterjee, Partha.1997.*The Nation and its Fragments.*Delhi: OUP.

Jeffrey, Robin.1992.*Politics, Women and Well-being How Kerala Became 'A Model'*. New Delhi: Oxford University Press.

Nigam, Aditya. 2000.'Secularism, Modernity, Nation: An Epistemology of The Dalit Critique', *Economic and Political Weekly*, Vol. 35, No. 48, November 25-Decemeber 1, pp. 4256-4268.

Vora, Rajendra and Feldhaus, Anne. Ed. 2006.*Region, Culture, and Politics in India.*New Delhi: Manohar.

Index